A Wee Worship Book

A Wee Worship Book

Fifth Incarnation

WILD GOOSE RESOURCE GROUP

**Wild Goose Publications
Wild Goose Resource Group**

First published 2015, reprinted 2016, 2017 and later

ISBN 978-1-84952-322-6

Text, music engravings, cover image & design
© 2015 Wild Goose Resource Group,
c/o Iona Community, Glasgow, Scotland.
www.wildgoose.scot

John L. Bell & Graham Maule/Wild Goose Resource Group
have asserted their rights
under the Copyright, Designs & Patents Act 1988,
to be identified as the authors of this work.

Published by Wild Goose Publications,
21 Carlton Court, Glasgow G5 9JP, Scotland.
www.ionabooks.com

Wild Goose Publications is the publishing division
of the Iona Community.
Scottish Charity No. SC003794.
Limited Company Reg.No. SC096243.

The Wild Goose is a Celtic symbol of the Holy Spirit.

All rights reserved.
No part of this publication may be reproduced in any form
or by any means, including photocopying
or any information storage or retrieval system,
without written permission from the publishers.

A catalogue record of this book is available from the British Library.

The publishers gratefully acknowledge the support of
the Drummond Trust, 3 Pitt Terrace, Stirling FK8 2EY.

Printed by Bell & Bain, Thornliebank, Glasgow

Contents

9	**Introduction**
11	**Regarding the Liturgies**
16	**How To Use This Book**

The Liturgies

19	**Morning Liturgy A**
26	**Morning Liturgy B**
31	**Morning Liturgy C**
38	**Morning Liturgy D**
43	**Morning Liturgy E**
51	**Morning Liturgy F**
56	**Evening Liturgy A**
62	**Evening Liturgy B**
68	**Evening Liturgy C**
71	**Evening Liturgy D**
76	**Evening Liturgy E**
82	**Evening Liturgy F**
87	**A Liturgy for Holy Communion**
87	Alternative prefaces
95	Alternative Communion prayers
100	Alternative invitational sentences

Appendix

103	**A: Affirmations of Belief**
103	Affirming the Trinitarian
104	Affirming the Global Church
105	Affirming the Church's Mission
107	Celebrating the Ministry of Jesus

Contents

108	**B: Songs**
108	Come, bring your burdens to God
109	Gloria (Iona)
110	Come, Holy Spirit
111	Through our lives and by our prayers
112	Alleluia (Greenbelt 10)
113	Kyrie (Maurs)
114	Glory and gratitude and praise
115	On God alone I wait silently
116	Peace I leave
117	Take, O take me as I am
118	Listen, Lord
119	This is the body of Christ
120	Come to me
121	Listen to the Word
122	**The Wild Goose Resource Group**
122	**Wild Goose Resource Group Titles**

Introduction

The maxim 'If it's not broken, don't fix it' might be applied to worship as much as to car maintenance; and with some justification. Words which are repeatedly said or sung in a communal setting gather to themselves depth, association and sentiment which makes us reluctant to have them replaced.

If worship were simply an exercise in self-gratification, the same prayers and songs could be confidently sung for ever. But such texts have two further effects of which we must take account.

Firstly they shape what we believe. That being so, we have to ensure that what is said or sung accords with revealed truth. Hence only to thank God for the beauty of the earth may have been appropriate a century ago. But now the extent by which humans endanger the natural order requires us to pray more about guardianship than admiration when it comes to creation. Therefore there must always be new texts which deal with realities and perceptions which older texts, written in a very different day, could not be expected to represent.

But more, what we say and sing is a gift to God; and God deserves more than an unchanging diet of prayer. This is not to discount the continuing spiritual and aesthetic worth of some of what was said and sung in the past. However, as with our friends and relatives, the same gift on every occasion does not indicate or guarantee a deepening of affection.

While the established churches are often hesitant to 'experiment', those of us who work nearer the fringe, and are aware of how disenchanting dull liturgy can be to insiders and outsiders alike, cannot be complacent. So we offer this book in its fifth edition, with material most of which has been developed and revised in the decade since the fourth edition was published. Very little that appears in the fourth edition has been carried into the fifth and we still regard the previous book as having continuing use and value.

We record our gratitude to those who have helped us shape and amend these liturgies, as we are also grateful to God from whom all blessings flow and to whom all that is contained here is offered.

John Bell
Graham Maule
Wild Goose Resource Group
December 2014

Regarding the Liturgies

The following are some new features in this book which deserve a short introduction.

1. Silence & (Pause)

Throughout the liturgies you will find both 'Silence' and '(Pause)'. These are not commands but suggestions.

Too often in worship, streams of words may titillate our ears, but give us little time to pause to reflect. Prayers which are led on our behalf only become our prayers when we are consciously enabled, as a result of the offered words, to present our own thoughts or wonderment to God. Liturgy is the bones; the worshippers have to supply the flesh. Hence the stop signs. A silence may be a minute or longer, a pause can be 10 to 20 seconds.

2. Psalms

We have included several of these which can be used, substituted or omitted. In most cases they offer a paraphrase rather than a literal translation. This is not to devalue the original text, but to indicate what translators know too well – that poetry in one language cannot be rendered word for word in translation. The versions supplied here were prepared keeping in mind that they were intended for public use and not private study. Therefore rhythm, required for shared speech, has been prominent in our thinking.

3. Liturgies drawing on *Carmina Gadelica*

The term 'Celtic' has become, in some places, a surrogate adjective for 'alternative'. We actually don't know very much about the

Celtic past in Scotland, nor do we have many documents dating from the great era of monastic evangelism.

But we do have a very interesting collection of songs, prayers and sayings called *Carmina Gadelica*. This material was gathered by Alexander Carmichael, an itinerant tax-collector, as he travelled through the highlands and islands at the end of the 19th century. It consists primarily of devotional and wisdom material passed down through the generations among Gaelic-speaking lay people, the overwhelming majority of whom could not read or write. This source material is therefore more authentically Celtic than much which has claimed that mantle in recent years.

Two liturgies have been constructed from material in Carmichael's collection, but they should not be regarded as historic examples of ancient corporate prayer. Most of the items that Carmichael collected were personal. Here, original poems or prayers are sometimes quoted verbatim; more often the texts draw on the ethos and the language of these people who singularly in the religious traditions of the world bear witness to lively faith which of necessity was often nurtured in situations where – as in some communities today – the presence of a priest or minister could not be guaranteed.

4. Affirmations of faith

From time to time, people may like to say in a condensed form what they believe. The affirmations in this book have all been used in different contexts and can be fitted into liturgies ad lib. But please do not regard them as creeds; they are only temporary expedients.

5. Scriptural reflections

Preaching a sermon or homily is only one way of opening the scripture. It is a model which not everyone can emulate. So here we suggest ways in which, should people want to reflect on the Word of God, it can be done more participatively. But please note that this does not require every worshipper to say something. Worship should not be coercive.

The methods of reflection suggested below are not based on a 'right answers' mentality. The leader is not the expert who has to judge whether contributions are correct or not. The reader facilitates a conversation where people explore the scripture rather than define its meaning.

Please remember, the Bible is a book of public truth, meant to be read to a listening people. Because reading the Bible in worship is not necessarily 'Bible study', we anticipate that the majority of worshippers should listen while one person reads and then trust their experience and intuition, as much as their intellect, to help understand the passage. If they want to check the *NRSV* against *The Good News*, let them do that at home.

(a) Remembering the story

When the passage of scripture to be read may fairly be regarded as well known, begin by asking participants to recall the story from memory and tell it to each other in as accurate a chronology as possible. This may be done first in small groups and shared in plenary, or it may be a purely plenary activity.

Then invite the participants to listen carefully as the passage is read and note what they did *not* remember. Thereafter in plenary or groups they should reflect on the importance of the details they had forgotten and perhaps ponder why these were not remembered.

(b) Why is it here?

There are many stories in the Hebrew Scriptures (Old Testament) which seem strange to our ears. The book of Judges is full of them. If the passage to be read seems of this sort, have it read twice and after the first reading say:

'We're going to hear this again, and afterwards we'll share with each other our response to this question: 'Out of all that God could have inspired to be included in the Bible, how come this story was selected?'

Then have it read again, ask the question and get people to turn to each other in small groups and converse. After five minutes, ask what kind of responses people made. And that's all. No need for a neat conclusion. Just thank participants for opening the Word.

(c) Right of reply

Given that most of the letters in the New Testament were written by Paul or others to specific churches, we might after hearing such a portion of scripture ask each other:

> i) What might have been happening to prompt this letter?
>
> ii) If Paul – or whoever – wrote this to our church, what might we reply?

Read the passage a second time before initiating the conversation.

(d) If I had been there . . .

A reading which refers to an incident involving several people may be followed by this question:

> 'If you had been there, and could ask a question of any of the people in the story, who would you want to speak to and what would you ask?'

(e) How will we change?

This, first experienced at Mass in a Roman Catholic church in Brussels, involves a passage from the Gospels. Most people will be familiar with texts from the Gospel, but perhaps not with this question:

> 'If this is the Gospel of our Lord which is meant to change

our lives, how should our lives change, now that we have heard the Gospel?'

Again, people speak in groups to each other for five or so minutes and then no 'reporting back'. The leader might simply ask if anything said in the groups might be worth sharing with everyone. He or she may then add a perspective from his/ her own experience or learning.

(f) Reflective silence

There is nothing wrong with sharing three or four minutes in reflective silence after a passage has been read, as long as people are told that is going to happen and for how long. In such a case this prayer may be used to begin and end the silence:

> Speak, God, to our listening;
> speak, God, to our thinking;
> speak to our soul's deep understanding

6. Standing and sitting

Depending on the place and the people, different parts of all these liturgies may be read sitting or standing. Where possible at least the opening and closing responses and hymns should be shared, and those who are able are invited to stand.

How To Use This Book

1. Don't say, 'I'll try the first three pages and see if they work.' Read through the whole book to discover the variety of material.

2. Don't say, 'I could never use this on Sunday with my people. They're not ready for it.'

   That sentiment is normally expressed by liturgical megalomaniacs whose umbilical cords are tied to their denominational Prayer Book, and to timid ministerial souls who trust neither themselves nor their congregation. (No, that's a bit too strong, but we're not used to being discreet.)

   This is not a substitute for what is used at the 10 o'clock mass or the 11 o'clock service. Although material may be used on such occasions, everything here was conceived for occasions *other than* Sunday mornings, and leadership is intended to be shared *among participants*, rather than led by one person.

3. Don't anticipate that one leader will do everything. In any liturgy there may be up to four or five leaders or readers. People will feel more comfortable with the words if they have had a chance to rehearse.

   (Did we say 'rehearse'? Yes we did.)

   Priests and ministers may be used to speaking in public and doing things at the last minute. But for people whose primary calling is not to ordained ministry, it is important that they should be able to become familiar with the words so that they can read them with confidence and conviction.

   Thus a complete novice might be asked to read the opening or closing responses which are usually short. On a future occasion he or she may do something more substantial. The role which most requires someone with sensitivity and experience is that of the leader who enables the scriptural reflections detailed above.

4. Don't be a fundamentalist in the use of this book. It is perfectly possible to omit, amend or add to what appears on the pages if a situation requires it.

5. Consider how people are going to sit. We prefer to gather sitting in a circle, semi-circle or three-sided formation.

   (Note: men should read the last sentence twice.)

   It is our experience of working for over 25 years on every continent that men much prefer people to sit in straight lines facing the front as an audience, rather than sit in a formation where all can see each other: God calls us to participate as a community, not to spectate as strangers.

6. Where some liturgical action is suggested – like lighting a candle – try it even if you are a born-again Calvinist with a deep emotional affection for electric lights. In worship as elsewhere, actions can often speak more loudly than words.

7. Sing. We include only short songs or chants in the Appendix, otherwise this would be the Gargantuan Worship Book. So use other books for hymns or songs. And don't feel there has to be a musician to accompany you. All of God's children have a voice, but many of us have lost the confidence to use it. And the only way to regain that confidence is . . . to sing.

8. Because this book, like its predecessor, might be used in sitting rooms and open spaces, decisions whether to stand or sit should be made in situ.

9. As much as possible, we have tried to make the language for humanity inclusive, and the language for God is mostly gender free. However the word 'Lord' is occasionally used, for the simple reason that there are significant cultures – especially

African American – in which this term is exclusively kept for God and Jesus 'because there is no other Lord'.

However, taking St Paul's advice to heart, we would rather the term be changed in contexts where not to would cause offence.

10. As with the Angelus bell, nine is enough.

Morning Liturgy A

Opening responses

Leader: O God, you summon the day to dawn;
you teach the morning to waken the earth.
ALL: GREAT IS YOUR NAME,
GREAT IS YOUR LOVE.

Leader: For you the valleys will sing for joy,
the trees of the field shall clap their hands.
ALL: GREAT IS YOUR NAME,
GREAT IS YOUR LOVE.

Leader: To you the monarchs of earth shall bow,
the poor and the persecuted shall shout for joy:
ALL: GREAT IS YOUR NAME,
GREAT IS YOUR LOVE.

Leader: Your love and justice shall last for ever,
fresh as the morning, sure as the sunrise.
ALL: GREAT IS YOUR NAME,
GREAT IS YOUR LOVE.

Song *or* Hymn

Prayer

Leader: Let us pray.

From before the world began
and after the end of eternity,
you are God.

From the sea bursting from its womb
to the wind ceasing from its chase,
you are God.

In the vastness of the universe
and the forgotten corners of our hearts,
you are God.

ALL: **YOU ARE OUR GOD,
AND WE BLESS YOU.**

Leader: Because the world is beautiful,
and beauty is a tender thing,
and we are caretakers of creation,
we need you, God.

ALL: **WE NEED YOU, GOD.**

Leader: Because human knowledge seems endless,
the world is our oyster
and we do not know what we do not know,
we need you, God.

ALL: **WE NEED YOU, GOD.**

Leader: Because we can live without you
and are free to go against you
and could worship our wisdom alone,
we need you, God.

ALL: **WE NEED YOU, GOD.**

Leader: Because you came among us
and sat beside us
and heard us speak and saw us ignore you
and healed our pain and let us wound you
and loved us to the end
and triumphed over all our hatred,
we need you, God.

ALL: **WE NEED YOU, GOD.**

Leader: Because you, not we, are God,
we need you, God.
ALL: WE NEED YOU, GOD.

    (Pause)

Leader: Listen, for the God who created us says,

'Do not be afraid,
for I have redeemed you;
I have called you by name:
you are mine.

'You are precious to me.
I love you,
I honour you,
I am with you.'

    (Pause)

So we respond:
ALL: MAKER OF ALL,
WE ARE YOUR CHILDREN,
THE CREATURES OF YOUR KINDNESS,
THE BEARERS OF YOUR IMAGE.

THIS DAY,
WE WILL WALK BY YOUR LIGHT,
FOLLOW YOUR SON.
AND LIVE BY YOUR SPIRIT,

THIS DAY,
WE WILL NOT OFFER TO YOU
OFFERINGS THAT COST US NOTHING.
FOR THIS IS THE DAY
THAT THE LORD HAS MADE;
WE WILL REJOICE AND BE GLAD IN IT.
AMEN.

Psalm 8

Leader: O Lord our God,
how glorious is your name in all the earth;
your majesty is praised above the heavens.
ALL: ON THE LIPS OF CHILDREN AND BABIES,
YOU HAVE FOUND PRAISE
TO FOIL YOUR ENEMIES,
TO SILENCE THE FOE AND THE REBEL.

Leader: When I see the heavens, the work of your hands,
the moon and stars which you arranged,
what are human beings
that you should remember them,
mere mortals
that you have time for them?
ALL: YOU HAVE MADE THEM
IN YOUR OWN IMAGE
AND CROWNED THEM
WITH GLORY AND HONOUR;
YOU APPOINTED THEM GUARDIANS
OF ALL YOU CREATED;
ALL THINGS ARE KEPT IN THEIR CARE.

Leader: All of them, sheep and cattle,
yes, even the savage beasts,
birds of the air, and fish
that make their way through the waters.
ALL: O LORD, OUR GOD,
HOW GLORIOUS IS YOUR NAME
IN ALL THE EARTH.

A reading from Holy Scripture

Reader: Listen for God's Word to God's people.

(Reading)

Reader: For the Word of God in scripture,
for the Word of God among us,
for the Word of God within us,
ALL: THANKS BE TO GOD.

Reflection *(see page 12, section 5) and/ or* **Silence**

Prayers of concern

Leader: Let us pray.

We cannot escape you
nor will we resist you;
for though your ways are not our ways
nor are your thoughts our thoughts,
it is on your Word and will
that all life depends.

You convert wrong into right;
therefore we trust you,
and so we pray:
God of justice,
ALL: SHOW YOURSELF.

Leader: Where the hungry go unfed,
while the privileged gorge themselves;
where the poor go begging
while the rich amass greater fortunes;
where tyrants have bitten the dust
but their successors prove no better;
God of justice,
ALL: SHOW YOURSELF.

Leader:	Where the prisoner is not prepared for freedom and the refugee is not accorded dignity; where those who are disadvantaged are excluded and those who are disabled are left on the margins; where gender, race or religion are grounds for suspicion, or confer unmerited privilege; God of justice,
ALL:	SHOW YOURSELF.
Leader:	To those who speak for the voiceless and defend the persecuted, to those who protest for a fairer world and practise simpler living, to those who share their faith in Jesus in places where faith is suspected; God of justice,
ALL:	SHOW YOURSELF.
Leader:	And to us, that we might serve and love you with body, soul and mind; God of justice,
ALL:	SHOW YOURSELF.
Leader:	God, hear our prayer and make us willing agents of your gracious purposes, in Jesus' name.
ALL:	AMEN.

Song *or* Hymn

Closing responses

Leader:	From where we are to where you need us,
ALL:	JESUS, NOW LEAD ON.

Leader: From the familiarity of what we know
to the wonder of what you will reveal,
ALL: JESUS, NOW LEAD ON.

Leader: To transform the fabric of this world
until it is resembles the shape of your kingdom,
ALL: JESUS, NOW LEAD ON.

Leader: Because good things have been prepared
for those who love God,
ALL: JESUS, NOW LEAD ON.

Morning Liturgy B

Opening responses

Leader: Way beyond all journeying,
Truth behind all mystery,
Life within all living:
ALL: WE PRAISE YOU.

Leader: Salve for every soreness,
mender of every brokenness,
midwife of a better future:
ALL: WE PRAISE YOU.

Leader: Ground of all being,
judge of all nations,
conscience of the universe,
ALL: WE PRAISE YOU.

Leader: Maker, Redeemer,
confessor, companion,
befriender, inspirer,
God beyond all names,
ALL: WE PRAISE YOU.

Song *or* **Hymn**

Prayer

Leader: Let us pray.

Because God is good,
and has intended us to share that goodness,
we open ourselves
to nothing less than transformation
as together we say:
ALL: HOLY GOD,
HOLY AND MIGHTY,
HOLY AND IMMORTAL
HAVE MERCY ON US.

Leader: You are the Word behind all words,
the calm at the core of the storm,
the energy that sustains creation.

You are present
in the pain behind the tears,
the laughter in the eyes,
the yearning in the heart.
All these you share,
yet your gift to us is much more.

So, open us up, Lord,
we whose lives are locked,
whose thoughts are well rehearsed,
whose prayer is predictable.

Open us up to depths we have not explored,
truths we have avoided,
paths we have not followed,
beauty we have yet to admire.

And open us up to Jesus,
in whom all things are held together for God
and for our good.
ALL: AMEN.

Psalm 67

Leader: May God be gracious to us and bless us,
may God cause his face to shine on us.
ALL: MAY GOD'S PURPOSE
BE KNOWN ON EARTH,
GOD'S SAVING POWER
AMONG THE NATIONS.

Leader: Let the people praise you, O God;
let all the people praise you.
ALL: LET THE NATIONS REJOICE
WITH SHOUTS OF GLADNESS,
FOR YOU JUDGE HUMANITY WITH FAIRNESS.

Leader: Let the people praise you, O God;
let all the people praise you.
ALL: MAY THE EARTH YIELD ITS HARVEST;
MAY GOD GRANT US ALL A BLESSING;
MAY THE WORLD STAND IN AWE
AND IN PRAISE OF ITS MAKER.

A reading from Holy Scripture

Reader: A reading from the book/ the gospel of ...

(Reading)

Reader: The Word of God for the people of God.
ALL: THANKS BE TO GOD.

Reflection *(see page 12, section 5) and/ or* **Silence**

Prayers of concern

Leader: Let us pray.

Because you, God, love the world,
because in Christ you walked it,
we dare to pray:
God, send your spirit;
ALL: RENEW THE LIFE OF THE EARTH.

Leader: To connect the words of ancient scripture
to the life of the world today;
to let the urgent summons of Jesus
surpass our reticence to respond,
God, send your spirit:
ALL: RENEW THE LIFE OF THE EARTH.

Leader: To awaken the minds of those in power
to the realities of those they govern;
to confront the arrogance of the privileged
with the vulnerability of the poor,
God, send your spirit;
ALL: RENEW THE LIFE OF THE EARTH.

Leader: To engage the fragile state of the planet
with those who carelessly abuse it;
to let the pain of those who are hurting
awaken the caring potential in the healthy,
God, send your spirit;
ALL: RENEW THE LIFE OF THE EARTH.

Leader: To eradicate the distance
between our convictions and commitments,
    our potentials and our performance,
    our prayers and our politics,
    our faith and our discipleship,
God, send your spirit;
ALL: RENEW THE LIFE OF THE EARTH.

Leader: Convince us, gracious God,
that matter matters
and that all is up for redemption.
And since in Jesus
you destined all to be changed and made new,
enable us to be agents of your purpose.
We pray in Jesus' name.
ALL: AMEN.

Song *or* Hymn

Closing responses

Leader: Is it true that God loves the world?
ALL: AMEN.
THIS IS TRUE.

Leader: Is it true that God loves all people?
ALL: AMEN.
THIS IS TRUE.

Leader: Is it true that Jesus came to make all things new?
ALL: AMEN.
THIS IS TRUE.

Leader: Then let us go
as those whom God has called,
to bear witness to the love and justice of heaven,
to be beacons of light
and signs of transformation,
for of such is the kingdom of heaven.
ALL: AMEN.

Morning Liturgy C

Opening responses

Leader: In the beginning,
 before time, before people,
 before the world began,
ALL: GOD WAS.

Leader: Here and now,
 among us, beside us,
 clearer than air, closer than breathing,
ALL: GOD IS.

Leader: In all that is to come,
 when we have turned to dust
 and human knowledge has been completed,
ALL: GOD WILL BE.

Leader: Not despairing of earth, but delighting in it,
 not condemning the world, but redeeming it
 through Jesus Christ,
 by the power of the Holy Spirit,
ALL: GOD WAS,
 GOD IS,
 GOD WILL BE.

Song *or* Hymn

Prayer

Leader: Let us pray.

Holy and gracious God,
we live in a world of wonder,
conceived by your divine imagination.
The universe is your creation
born out of love and generosity.

Hallowed be your name.
ALL: HALLOWED BE YOUR NAME.

Leader: Through centuries of thought and searching,
through law and wisdom, insight and experience,
your will and purpose were gradually glimpsed
until, in Jesus, all that was hidden was revealed,
and you let earth be touched by heaven.

Hallowed be your name.
ALL: HALLOWED BE YOUR NAME.

Leader: In the beauty of the earth,
in the silence of our hearts,
in the community of your church,
in all works of grace and kindness,
in forgiving from the heart
and in worship from the soul,
your Spirit confirms the truth by which we live.

Hallowed be your name.
ALL: HALLOWED BE YOUR NAME.

Leader: If, knowing this,
we have failed to love you, our Maker,
been hesitant to follow your Son,
and suspected the power of your Spirit,
Lord, have mercy.
ALL: LORD, HAVE MERCY.

Leader:	If we have desired comfort more than devotion,
	if we have satisfied our wants
	more than we have served your will,
	if we have worshipped a lesser god
	and gone for an easier gospel,
	Christ, have mercy.
ALL:	CHRIST, HAVE MERCY.
Leader:	If, in the face of your openness,
	we have privatised our wealth,
	limited our company to those like us,
	restricted our conversation
	to matters of no consequence,
	and in all this compromised our integrity
	and lost faith in our faith,
	Lord, have mercy.
ALL:	LORD, HAVE MERCY.

(Pause)

Leader:	Forgive us, O God,
	but not to ease our consciences
	until we feel penitent again.
	Forgive us,
	so that we may have no defence against your will;
	and then make us friends of your purpose
	and worthy companions of Jesus,
	in whose name we pray.
ALL:	AMEN.

Psalm 95

Reader:	Come, let us sing a joyful song to God, shout in triumph to the rock of our salvation.
ALL:	LET US ENTER GOD'S PRESENCE WITH GRATITUDE AND WORSHIP WITH HEARTFELT JOY.
Reader:	The Lord is a great God, greater than every idol.
ALL:	THE DEPTHS OF THE EARTH ARE IN GOD'S CARE, AS ARE THE HIGHEST MOUNTAINS.
Reader:	The sea belongs to God whose hands carved out the land.
ALL:	LET US DRAW NEAR TO GOD IN WORSHIP; AND COME BEFORE OUR MAKER, FOR WE ARE THE FLOCK WHOM GOD SHEPHERDS.

A reading from Holy Scripture

Reader:	Hear the Word of God.
ALL:	OUR EARS AND HEARTS ARE OPEN.

(Reading)

Reader:	Give thanks to the One whose Word is life.
ALL:	BLESSED BE GOD FOR EVER.

Reflection *(see page 12, section 5) and/ or* **Silence**

Prayers of concern

Leader: Let us pray.

May it not be long, Lord ...

May it not be long
before the world we pray for
and the world we inhabit
are one.

May it not be long
before the domination of wealth over want,
    white over black,
    man over woman,
    the privileged over the poor
are facts of history,
not facts of life.

ALL: MAY IT NOT BE LONG.

Leader: May it not be long, Lord,
before the earth no longer suffers
through human selfishness,
so that the valleys can sing again,
the meadows laugh
and barren places burst into bloom.

ALL: MAY IT NOT BE LONG.

Leader: May it not be long, Lord,
before economic power comes only
with accountability,
and money and taxation are wedded
to just purposes.

ALL: MAY IT NOT BE LONG.

Leader: May it not be long, Lord,
before the countries
which the West once evangelised
show us the larger Christ
we have yet to encounter.
ALL: MAY IT NOT BE LONG.

Leader: May it not be long, Lord,
before we vacate the safe refuges
of pessimism and cynicism,
and find wells of hope
deeper than shallow pools of optimism.
ALL: MAY IT NOT BE LONG.

Leader: May it not be long, Lord,
before we feel ourselves directly addressed
by your voice
as those first disciples did,
who heard you summon the strangest of people
to the greatest of callings.
ALL: MAY IT NOT BE LONG.

Leader: May it not be long, Lord.

And to enable that day to come soon,
raise up for us prophets
who will give us new sight for better seeing.

Raise up for us prophets
who will increase our altruism
and diminish our greed.
Raise up for us prophets
who will spell out
that God has no favourite race
nor heaven a favoured language.

Raise up for us prophets
who, in their own person,
will bridge the gaps through which too many fall.

Raise up for us prophets
who will make clear for our day
the truths Jesus said in his,
and who will speak with the urgency of those
who have glimpsed the coming of the Lord.

ALL: AND IF YOU WILL NOT RAISE UP
FOR US PROPHETS,
THEN RAISE UP IN US
THAT HOLY RESTLESSNESS
TO GET YOUR WORK DONE
AND YOUR PEOPLE SAVED,
FOR JESUS' SAKE.
AMEN.

Song *or* **Hymn**

Closing responses

Leader: Now may God
who gives seed to the sower
and corn to the reaper,
give to us all that we need
to produce a good harvest.

ALL: MAY GOD MAKE US FERTILE
IN FAITH, HOPE AND LOVE,
AND TAKE US OUT WITH JOY
AND LEAD US ON IN PEACE,
AS SIGNS OF THE FRUITFULNESS OF HEAVEN.
AMEN.

Morning Liturgy D

This liturgy opens with words shared between men and women. If the company is of one gender, then make a creative change such as 'those under/ over forty' – or 'those who drink tea/ drink coffee at breakfast'.

At the end, there is an invitation for people to join hands at the close of worship. This is not mandatory, but it does celebrate that we are meant to be a joined-up body.

Opening responses

Leader:	Christ is like a single body which has many parts.
ALL:	IT IS STILL ONE BODY THOUGH EVERY PART IS DIFFERENT.
Leader:	Therefore the foot cannot say,
Men:	I AM NOT PART OF THE BODY;
Leader:	nor can the ear say,
Women:	I AM NOT PART OF THE BODY.
Leader:	The eye cannot say to the hand,
Men:	I DON'T NEED YOU;
Leader:	nor can the head say to the feet,
Women:	I DON'T NEED YOU.
Leader:	If one part suffers,
ALL:	ALL PARTS SHARE THE PAIN;
Leader:	if one part is praised,
ALL:	ALL PARTS SHARE THE JOY.
Leader:	Together, we are Christ's body:
ALL:	EACH ONE OF US IS A PART OF IT.

Song *or* Hymn

Prayer

Leader: Let us pray.

Gracious God,
if we came to your house,
we would find the door open,
because there are no closing hours
for the hospitality of heaven.

ALL: IF WE CAME TO YOUR HOUSE,
WE WOULD HEAR MANY ACCENTS,
OURS JUST ONE AMONG THEM,
FOR THERE IS NO FAVOURED NATION
IN THE COMMONWEALTH OF HEAVEN.

Leader: If we came to your house,
we would see people who never thought
they would be allowed in,
had entrance been by merit
rather than by your gracious invitation.

So, as we gather in Jesus' name,
let the characteristics you cherish
become evident in all we do and share together.

Gather into one
the glorious assortment of unlikes
which is your true church.

ALL: REVEAL WITHIN THIS COMMUNITY
WHAT WE MUST DO,
WHAT WE MUST HEAR,
AND WHO WE MUST WELCOME
IF WE ARE TO KNOW JESUS AMONG US.

Leader: God, give us the grace
to surrender our presumptions
as to what we should be or do;
and then amend our lives
until we become the people you intended.
ALL: AMEN.

Psalms 133 & 134

Reader: How good and how lovely it is
to live together in unity.
ALL: PRECIOUS IT IS, LIKE OIL,
POURED OUT TO ANOINT THE HEAD.

Reader: Unity is like the dew
falling on holy mountains.
ALL: WITH IT COMES GOD'S BLESSING:
LIFE FOR EVERMORE.

Reader: Come, bless the Lord, you servants
fulfilling God's commands;
ALL: LOVE AND PRAISE YOUR MAKER,
THE GOD OF HEAVEN AND EARTH.

A reading from Holy Scripture

Reader: Listen now for the voice of God
within the words of Scripture.

(Reading)

Reader: Heavenly words for earthly people;
ALL: THANKS BE TO GOD.

Reflection *(see page 12, section 5) and/ or* **Silence**

Prayer

Leader: Let us pray.

Before we leave this place,
a prayer for our own healing,
the healing of bodies which are sick,
or hearts that are weary,
or minds that are confused,
or imaginations that are overactive,
or memories which are menacing ...

(Pause)

God, in your mercy,
ALL: HEAR OUR PRAYER.

Leader: Before we leave this place,
a prayer for our own deepening –
in faith, hope and love,
in our life as a community of believers,
in our own walk with God ...

(Pause)

God, in your mercy,
ALL: HEAR OUR PRAYER.

Leader: Before we leave this place,
let us ask what God wants us to hear,
to have or to do,
and be open to receive it graciously ...

(Pause)

God, in your mercy,
ALL: HEAR OUR PRAYER.

Leader: For all that God gives to us, we say
ALL: THANK YOU.

Leader:	To all that God asks of us, we say
ALL:	YES,
Leader:	in Jesus' name,
ALL:	AMEN.

Song *or* Hymn

Blessing

Leader: Let us stand for a moment in silence
and value our souls,
our minds and our bodies
on which we will ask God's blessing.

   (ALL stand in silence)

Let the Body of Christ join hands.

   (ALL join hands)

May God bless us
in our bodies with health,
in our minds with understanding,
in our souls with the company of the Holy Spirit,
that together we may produce a harvest of light
to the glory of Christ our Saviour,
whose flesh we are,
whose name we bear,
whose love is all.

ALL: AMEN.

Morning Liturgy E

In terms of time, this is the longest of the morning liturgies. However, this does not imply that it should be galloped through, especially in the prayers for others when it would be helpful to leave a space for personal prayer between the words of the petition and the shared response.

Opening responses

Leader A: All you works of God,
 all you mighty heavens;
Leader B: all you angels of light,
 all you saints in glory –
ALL: WORSHIP AND PRAISE YOUR MAKER.

Leader A: All you heavenly bodies,
 sun and moon and stars;
Leader B: all you earthly weathers –
 wind and rain and thunder –
ALL: WORSHIP AND PRAISE YOUR MAKER.

Leader A: Fire and searing heat,
 ice and deadly cold;
Leader B: light and deepest dark,
 endless nights and days –
ALL: WORSHIP AND PRAISE YOUR MAKER.

Leader A: Mountains and high hills,
 forests and tall trees:
Leader B: countless flowers and plants,
 waterfalls and streams –
ALL: WORSHIP AND PRAISE YOUR MAKER.

Leader A: Whales beneath the seas,
                 birds throughout the skies;
Leader B: all that leaps or crawls,
                 creatures wild and tame –
ALL: WORSHIP AND PRAISE YOUR MAKER.

Leader A: People, young and old,
                 children, women, men;
Leader B: all who do heaven's will,
                 all who love the Lord –
ALL: WORSHIP AND PRAISE YOUR MAKER.

Song *or* Hymn

Prayer

Leader: Let us pray.

             Eternal God,
             you do not need our praise.
             The world itself tells of your glory ...
             sunrise and birdsong,
             the ruggedness of landscape,
             the randomness of rain,
             beauty for the eye,
             nourishment for the body,
             music for the soul
               ... these all speak of your goodness
             these honour your name.

             You do not need our praise.

             Other places can do it better
             with finer music or fewer words,
             with centuries of tradition
             or buildings of rare beauty.

Other people can do it better,
where two or three are gathered
who live in poverty or under threat,
and who, despite all that oppresses them,
rejoice to be called your own.

What can we add
by way of magnificence or testimony
when these are more eloquent?

You do not need our praise,
but we need to praise you.
It is the yearning, the restlessness
which you have planted in us.
It is our desire for a true home
and unconditional acceptance
that brings us here.

All the rumours we have heard about you
are true:
> you love,
> you forgive,
> you transform.

And you know us ...
oh, how you know us.
You perceive what in us needs to be loved,
what in us needs to be forgiven,
and what in us needs to be changed.

We need no more words,
just penitence.

(Pause)

Leader:	Lord, have mercy on us.
ALL:	LORD, HAVE MERCY ON US.
Leader:	Christ, have mercy on us.
ALL:	CHRIST, HAVE MERCY ON US.
Leader:	Lord, have mercy on us.
ALL:	LORD, HAVE MERCY ON US

(Pause)

Leader: These are the words of Jesus.
They are strong and true, so believe them:

'I have come
that you may have life in all its fullness.'

'Go in peace; your sins are forgiven:
Come, each one, and follow me.'

(Pause)

Now, God,
help us to live as a forgiven people –
visibly different,
gloriously free,
for Jesus' sake.

ALL: AMEN.

Psalm 65

Leader: You are God, our deliverer,
in whom all put their trust:
ALL: ALL WHO LIVE ON THE EARTH;
ALL BEYOND THE HORIZON.

Morning Liturgy E

Leader: By great skill and untold strength,
 you fixed the mountains in place;
ALL: YOU CALM THE RAGING SEAS
 AND QUIETEN WARRING NATIONS.

Leader: People throughout the world
 stand in awe of your skill.
ALL: LANDS TO EAST AND WEST
 GRATEFULLY SING YOUR PRAISE.

Leader: You care for the life of the world,
 forever tending the ground.
ALL: THUS YOU PREPARE ITS PRODUCE,
 THE CROPS THAT FEED ITS PEOPLE.

Leader: You water and level the earth,
 blessing its seasonal growth;
ALL: YOU CROWN THE YEAR
 WITH YOUR GOODNESS;
 THE EARTH EXHIBITS YOUR BOUNTY.

Leader: The open pastures are lush,
 the hills are wreathed with joy.
ALL: THE MEADOWS ARE CLOTHED WITH SHEEP,
 THE VALLEYS BURST INTO SONG.

A reading from Holy Scripture

Reader: Listen for the One
 whose thoughts are not our thoughts,
 whose ways are not our ways.

 (Reading)

Reader: The Word of God for the people of God.
ALL: THANKS BE TO GOD.

Reflection *(see page 12, section 5) and/ or* **Silence**

Prayers for others

Leader: Let us pray.

For the healing of bodies we pray:
for a holy healing
which deals with both pain and its causes;
for healing
which leads to a new love for the body,
a new care for the body;
and also, where mortal life wearies for the end,
for the healing of death.

(Pause)

Lord, hear us.
ALL: LORD, GRACIOUSLY HEAR US.

Leader: For the healing of minds we pray:
for a holy healing
which deals with memories as well as madness,
abuse as well as anxiety,
depression as well as dementia,
stigma as well as the suffering of a tortured mind;
and also,
where people have been hurt by religion,
for the healing of faith.

(Pause)

Lord, hear us.
ALL: LORD, GRACIOUSLY HEAR US.

Leader: For the healing of relationships we pray:
for a holy healing
which will not make things nice,
but will make things possible;
for the mending of love
which has been fractured,
for the cherishing of those
whose true sexuality has been deemed aberrant,
and for the holding in brokenness
of those for whom love has been undermined
by deceit.

(Pause)

Lord, hear us.
ALL: LORD, GRACIOUSLY HEAR US.

Leader: For the healing of our world we pray:
for a holy healing,
for the tearing down of cruel barriers
and the building of bridges for peace;
for the ending of needless exploitation
and the growth of reverence for our planet;
for replacing what the wealthy want
with an abundance of what the world needs.

(Pause)

Lord, hear us.
ALL: LORD, GRACIOUSLY HEAR US.

Leader: So we pray,
so we trust,
so we will do
in Jesus' name.
ALL: AMEN.

Song *or* Hymn

Closing responses

Leader: Prepare the way of the Lord;
ALL: MAKE A PATH FOR OUR GOD IN THE DESERT.

Leader: Each valley shall be exalted;
ALL: EVERY MOUNTAIN AND HILL BE LAID LOW.

Leader: The crooked shall be made straight;
ALL: ROUGH PLACES SHALL BECOME PLAIN.

Leader: The glory of the Lord shall be revealed;
ALL: ALL PEOPLE SHALL SEE IT TOGETHER.

Leader: This is the will of the Lord:
ALL: GOD'S PROMISE SHALL BE FULFILLED.

Morning Liturgy F

This liturgy draws on various texts from Carmina Gadelica. *See page 11, section 3.*

Opening responses

Leader: May God be among us throughout this day.
ALL: AMEN.

Leader: May Christ be beside us throughout this day.
ALL: AMEN.

Leader: May the Spirit be within us throughout this day.
ALL: AMEN.

Leader: May we, as God's people,
be at one with the saints in heaven
and live in harmony with the Blessed Three
to whom be praise and glory for ever.
ALL: AMEN.

Song *or* Hymn

Prayer

Leader: Let us pray.

Each thing we have received —
ALL: FROM GOD IT CAME.

Leader: Each thing we enjoy —
ALL: FROM GOD IT COMES.

Leader: Each thing we pray for –
ALL: FROM GOD IT WILL BE GIVEN.

Leader: God of life,
you are the source of all goodness
and the satisfaction of all our desires.

Our understanding of you is small;
increase it.
Our desire to do your will is weak;
enliven it.
The seed you have planted
has yet to bear fruit;
ripen it.

But first, create in us clean hearts
as, in your sight,
we unburden ourselves of guilt,
of anger,
of fear,
of pride,
of hardness of heart,
of weakness of intention.

(Pause)

Leader: Jesus, Son of Mary,
ALL: HAVE MERCY UPON US.

Leader: Jesus, Saviour of the World,
ALL: MAKE PEACE WITHIN US.

Leader: Christ, King of Glory,
ALL: BE WITH US AND FOR US
WHEREVER LIFE TAKES US.

Leader: In the common path of our calling
whether it be easy or uneasy to tread,
whether it be bright or dark to follow
let your perfect guidance protect us.

ALL:	BE A SHIELD AGAINST ALL THAT MIGHT DECEIVE US, BE A HEALER FOR ALL THAT MIGHT HARM US, BE A WITNESS OF ALL THAT MIGHT TROUBLE US, BE A FRIEND TO ALL WHO ARE DEAR TO US, THIS DAY AND UNTIL WE MEET IN GLORY. AMEN.

Psalm 19

Reader:	The heavens proclaim the glory of God, the sky displays God's artistry.
ALL:	ONE DAY COMMUNICATES WITH ANOTHER; NIGHT SHARES ITS KNOWLEDGE WITH NIGHT.
Reader:	This happens in absence of speech; creation requires no language.
ALL:	GOD'S PURPOSE IS SHOT THROUGH THE EARTH; GOD'S WISDOM THROUGHOUT THE WIDE WORLD.
Reader:	God placed in skies high above a tent for the bright shining sun.
ALL:	IT APPEARS LIKE A GROOM FOR HIS BRIDE; LIKE A CHAMPION, IT RUNS ITS FULL RACE.
Reader:	It rises and circles the earth;
ALL:	NOTHING MAY HIDE FROM ITS HEAT.
Reader:	The Law of the Lord is perfect, God's teaching revives the soul.
ALL:	GOD'S INSTRUCTIONS ARE STEADFAST AND SURE; THEY AIM TO MAKE SIMPLE FOLK WISE.

Reader: The guidance of God is good;
bringing joy to the humble in heart.
ALL: THE COMMANDMENTS OF GOD ARE CLEAR;
GOD'S WORD IS LIGHT TO THE EYES

A reading from Holy Scripture

Reader: Give us, O God,
as a morning meal,
the nourishment of your Word
to benefit our bodies, our minds,
our souls, our belief.

(Reading)

Let your Word live within us, faithful God
ALL: DAY BY DAY, NIGHT BY NIGHT,
IN OUR THINKING,
OUR SPEAKING,
OUR DOING,
OUR BELIEVING.

Prayers for others

Leader: O great and generous God,
graciously set your eye this day
on those who know their need of you
through pain,
through trouble,
through grief,
through their own fault.

(Pause)

Nurse the weak,
ALL: BANDAGE THE BROKEN,
CONSOLE THE DESOLATE,
FORGIVE THE PENITENT.

Leader: O Christ who shared our flesh,
graciously set your eye this day
on those who have no need for you
> through pride,
> through disappointment,
> through doubt,
> through the failure of false friends.

(Pause)

Soften the hardened heart,
ALL: CONFRONT THE ARROGANT WILL,
UNCOVER HIDDEN DEPTHS
AND THE TRUTH THAT SETS US FREE.

Leader: O Holy Spirit, breath of God,
move among us this day.

Open us to the beauty of the earth
so that we may become its servants.
Open us to the wonder of life
that we may recognise an angel at every corner.
Open to us the storehouse of your grace
and we will be made new for Jesus' sake.
ALL: AMEN.

Song *or* Hymn

Closing responses

Leader: Now may God who brought us
into the joyous light of this new day,
bring us to the guiding light of eternity.

ALL: GOD ABOVE US, GOD BENEATH US,
GOD BEHIND US, GOD BEFORE US,
GOD IN QUIETNESS, GOD IN DANGER,
GOD IN HEART OF FRIEND AND STRANGER.

Evening Liturgy A

It is particularly helpful to have people sitting in the round, with a table in their midst on which (optionally) may be placed the three symbols indicated in the opening responses. A chant – such as the Iona GLORIA – may be sung after each section as the symbols are placed. During the prayers for others, there is time for open prayer. This might be concluded by singing THROUGH OUR LIVES AND BY OUR PRAYERS, page 111.

Opening responses

Leader:	In the beginning when it was very quiet, the Word was with God.
ALL:	AND WHAT GOD WAS, THE WORD WAS.

(Here a Bible may be placed centrally)

Leader:	In the beginning when it was very dark, God said, 'Let there be light,'
ALL:	AND THERE WAS LIGHT.

(Here a lit candle may be placed centrally)

Leader:	When the time was right God sent the Son.
ALL:	HE CAME AMONG US, HE WAS ONE OF US.

(Here a cross may be placed centrally)

Silence

Song *or* Hymn

Prayer

Leader: Let us pray.

You keep us waiting ...
you, the God of all time,
want us to wait for the right time
in which to discover
who we are,
where we must go,
who will be with us,
and what we must do.

ALL: SO, THANK YOU ...
FOR THE WAITING TIME.

Leader: You keep us looking ...
you, the God of all space,
want us to look in the right and wrong places
for signs of hope,
for people who are hopeless,
for visions of a better world
which will appear among the disappointments
of the world we know.

ALL: SO, THANK YOU ...
FOR THE LOOKING TIME.

Leader: You keep us loving ...
you, the God whose name is love,
want us to be like you –
to love the loveless and the unloved and the unlovely;
to love without jealousy or design or threat;
and, most difficult of all,
to love ourselves.

ALL: SO, THANK YOU ...
FOR THE LOVING TIME.

Leader: And in all this,
you keep us ...
through hard questions with no easy answers,
through failing where we hoped to succeed
and making an impact
when we thought we were useless,
through the patience and encouragement
and love of others,
and through Jesus Christ and the Holy Spirit,
you
keep us.

ALL: SO, THANK YOU ...
FOR THE KEEPING TIME
AND FOR NOW AND FOR EVER.
AMEN.

Psalm 34

Reader: I will bless the Lord at all times;
God's praise will be always on my lips.
ALL: MY SOUL WILL GLORY IN THE LORD;
LET THE HUMBLE LISTEN AND REJOICE.

Reader: Together, let us praise God's greatness,
together, let us honour God's name.
ALL: I LOOKED FOR GOD AND GOD ANSWERED ME,
AND LIBERATED ME FROM ALL MY FEAR.

Reader: Those who look to God become radiant;
their faces need show no shame.
ALL: THIS POOR SOUL CRIED AND GOD HEARD ME
AND SAVED ME FROM ALL MY TROUBLES.

Reader: Fear God, you holy people;
those who show reverence will be satisfied.

ALL: PRINCES MAY LANGUISH AND HUNGER
BUT THOSE WHO SEEK GOD
LACK FOR NOTHING.

A reading from Holy Scripture

(The Text is read, after which the following is spoken)

Reader: The Word of the Lord is medicine for the soul.
ALL: THANKS BE TO GOD.
AMEN.

Silence *and/ or* **Reflection** *(see page 12, section 5)*

Prayers for others

Leader: Let us pray.

Let us pray for light ...
   where the dark is doubly dark;
   where wrong dresses up as right
   and even saints can be distracted;
   where life has gone into a tunnel
   and all that is known is confusing voices
   and stumbling blocks in the darkness;
   where faith and hope and love are in ashes,
   needing an angel to blow on them.

Let us pray for light.

(Open prayer – aloud or silent – which may be followed by a response or chant)

Let us pray for a word from the Lord ...
   where human words can no longer be trusted;
   where voices from the past echo loudly saying,
   'You are not one of us'
   or 'Keep quiet'
   or 'I do not need you any longer'
   or 'You never get it right';
   where the voice of the church has been like
   sweet and sour water from the same rock,
   saying 'Welcome,' and 'Watch it ...';
   where the voice of God has seemed silent
   or been submerged beneath jargon.

Let us pray for a word from the Lord.

(Open prayer, etc, as above)

Let us pray for a friend of God ...
   who will bring encouragement
   where there is despair;
   who will bring company
   where there is loneliness;
   who will listen
   where a hard truth has to be shared;
   who will bring change or conversion
   through kindness;
   who will speak truth to power;
   who will bring the gift
   which makes all the difference.

Let us pray for a friend of God ...

(Open prayer, etc, as above)

Help us, most Holy One,
to hear you
in the words of scripture
and also to recognise your accent
in the voices of the world.

ALL: HELP US TO SEE YOU
IN THE GOOD OTHERS DO
AND IN THE NEED
WHICH CALLS FOR LOVE OR JUSTICE.

Leader: Help us
to love you
and so to trust you
and follow you.

ALL: TAKE FROM US ANY DESIRE
FOR RECOGNITION OR REWARD,
AND REPLACE IT WITH THE QUIET JOY
WHICH COMES FROM KNOWING
THAT WE DO YOUR WILL
AMEN.

Song *or* Hymn

Closing responses

Leader: God of the watching ones,
the waiting ones,
the prayerful and positive ones,
the angels in heaven,
the child in the womb,
ALL: GIVE US YOUR BENEDICTION,
YOUR GOOD WORD FOR OUR SOULS
THAT WE MAY REST AND RISE
IN THE KINDNESS OF YOUR COMPANY.
AMEN.

Evening Liturgy B

Opening responses

Leader: Blessed be God
who creates out of nothing,
who shapes beauty out of chaos,
breathes life into dust,
delights in designing difference
and embodies in each human
the image of our Maker.

ALL: BLESSED BE GOD FOR EVER.

(As an alternative to the spoken response, an ALLELUIA or another chant may be sung)

Leader: Blessed be God
who gives each person a purpose:
calling the young for their energy
and the old for their wisdom;
refusing to discriminate
in terms of race, colour,
intellect or giftedness;
affirming forgotten worth,
identifying hidden potential,
redeeming deep regrets.

ALL: BLESSED BE GOD FOR EVER. *(Or as above)*

Leader: Blessed be God
who forsakes heaven
to live on earth,
who, in Jesus,
is truly flesh of our flesh
and bone of our bone,

vulnerable to pain, rumour and conflict,
open to question,
committed to heal,
sentenced to death,
destined for resurrection,
vindicating the power and the love of God
ever holy,
ever one.

ALL: BLESSED BE GOD FOR EVER. *(Or as above)*

Leader: Blessed be the Maker,
the Son and the Spirit
in our lives and our worship.
ALL: AMEN.

Song *or* Hymn

Prayer

Leader: Let us pray.

You have embodied us.

You, our wise creator,
have shaped us with bones
and coated us with flesh;
and in features as in voice
you have made each one unique.
You have embodied us.

Our body is a home we can never leave;
for though our hearts may take us to heaven
and our minds lead us to hell,
our feet are firmly grounded.
You have embodied us.

You have embodied us
and more than this,
you have made us your body
joining us to flesh and blood, hearts and minds,
purposes and passions not our own.

You have joined us
to the starving poor in India
and to the intelligentsia in the Vatican;
to Pentecostals in Zimbabwe
and Mennonites in Paraguay;
to threatened Christians in the Middle East
and respected believers in Cuba;
and to the widows and orphans whom Jesus loves,
and to the beggars and prostitutes
among whom Jesus sits throughout the world.

You have embodied us.
You are the womb from which all came,
you are the life on which all depends,
you are the destiny which lies before us,
you are the Eternal Word whom Jesus embodied.

So we trust you,
so we praise you.
ALL: AMEN.

Psalm 71

Leader: In you, O God, is my security;
let me never be put to shame.
ALL: BY YOUR SAVING POWER DELIVER ME,
HEAR ME AND KEEP ME SAFE.

Leader: Be a rock of refuge for me
to which I can always come.
ALL: KEEP ME SAFE
FROM THE POWER OF THE WICKED,
FROM THE GRASP OF THE CRUEL AND UNJUST.

Leader: In you, as long as I can remember,
my hope and my trust have been placed.
ALL: I HAVE LEANED ON YOU SINCE MY BIRTH,
SINCE YOU BROUGHT ME OUT OF THE WOMB.

Leader: Keep close when energy fails me
and I spend my last years on earth.
ALL: LET ME WAIT IN CONTINUAL HOPE
AND PRAISE YOU AGAIN AND AGAIN.

A reading from Holy Scripture

(The Text is read, after which the following is spoken)

Reader: For the Word of God in scripture,
for the Word of God among us,
for the Word of God within us.
ALL: THANKS BE TO GOD.

Silence *and/ or* **Reflection** *(see page 12, section 5)*

Prayer for ourselves

Leader: Let us pray.

Take our hands, Lord,
not to lift us out of the world,
but to lead us through it
as a mother fondly leads her son
and a father his daughter.

God, in your mercy,
ALL: HEAR OUR PRAYER.

Leader: Take from us the worn clothes of adulthood
and dress us up like children
so that we can dream and imagine and play again
without fear or contradiction.

God, in your mercy,
ALL: HEAR OUR PRAYER.

Leader: Speak to us in the silence we learn to cherish,
and let our conversation with you
move from formality to friendliness,
until all of life and all of us
become open to your Spirit.

God, in your mercy,
ALL: HEAR OUR PRAYER.

Leader: Graciously treasure us, Lord,
as a lover embraces the beloved.
Reveal to us in fond intimacy
all that you wish us to receive from you
and all you wish to receive from us.

God, in your mercy.
ALL: HEAR OUR PRAYER.

Leader: Give us a deep cherishing
where we have had our fill of shallow pleasures;
give us affection for ourselves
where we have neglected the beauty
which you planted in us;
give us love for you,
especially if respect is all we usually offer.

God, in your mercy.
ALL: HEAR OUR PRAYER.

Leader: And this night,
to those who are anxious bring calm,

ALL:	AND ENLIVEN THOSE IMPAIRED BY APATHY.
Leader: *ALL:*	To the sick in body, mind and spirit bring healing, AND TO THEIR CARERS BRING SKILL AND SENSITIVITY.
Leader: *ALL:*	To the abused bring safe affection, AND SEND AN ANGEL TO FORESTALL THEIR ABUSERS.
Leader: *ALL:*	To the war-torn and oppressed bring the dawn of a different day, AND TO THOSE WHO WIELD POWER GIVE THE WISDOM TO USE IT WISELY.
Leader: *ALL:*	And now we put into your hands, which cradle creation, our souls, our bodies, our hopes, our fears, our past and our future; for you alone are God from whom all goodness comes and through whom all life is made new. AMEN.

Song *or* Hymn

Closing responses

Leader: *ALL:*	For this time and this place and these people, MAY JESUS CHRIST BE PRAISED.
Leader: *ALL:*	By the faithful on earth and the saints in heaven, MAY JESUS CHRIST BE PRAISED.
Leader: *ALL:*	Through this night and at every day's dawning, MAY JESUS CHRIST BE PRAISED.

Evening Liturgy C

In this liturgy, which is more meditative than the others, it is suggested that two chants might be used. If this is to happen, make sure that people know the songs before starting, by having them sung through a couple of times in advance of worship.

Chant: VENI, SANCTE SPIRITUS/ *Taizé*
or COME, HOLY SPIRIT *(Page 110)*
or ON GOD ALONE I WAIT SILENTLY *(Page 115)*

Greeting

Leader: The Lord be with you.
ALL: AND ALSO WITH YOU.

Leader: May this time be good for us
in body, mind and spirit,
for we gather in the presence of God,
who made us and loves us
and will never leave us.
ALL: AMEN.

Prayer

Leader: Lord, teach us the silence of humility,
ALL: THE SILENCE OF WISDOM,
Leader: the silence of love,
ALL: THE SILENCE THAT SPEAKS WITHOUT WORDS,
Leader: the silence of faith.

Lord, teach us to silence our own hearts and minds
that we may listen
for the movement of your Spirit within us,

| | and treasure your presence
in the depths of our being. |
|--------|---|
| ALL: | AMEN. |

Silence

Chant *(As sung previously)* or Psalm 131

| Leader: | My heart, put away your false pride;
my eyes, do not look with disdain.
My ambition, forsake things beyond you;
my mind, find your proper proportion. |
|---------|---|
| ALL: | LORD, LET ME BE CALM AND QUIETENED,
AND HOLD TO YOU LIKE A CHILD
WHO CLINGS WITH DELIGHT TO HER MOTHER. |

A reading from Holy Scripture

Silence

Meditation

(A short silence should be kept after each of the 'times')

Leader: There is a time for every purpose under heaven
and a prayer for every person on earth:

...a time for those in physical pain or mental anguish;

...a time for the emotionally bruised and broken;

...a time for those who fear tomorrow;

...a time for those who have been blessed by today;

. . . a time for letting go or for picking up;

. . . a time for what we only share with God.

Chant: O LORD, HEAR MY PRAYER / *Taizé*
or UBI CARITAS ET AMOR / *Taizé*
or TAKE, O TAKE ME AS I AM / *WGRG, Iona*

Collect

Leader: Come to us, Holy God,
as you came to Mary,
purposefully.

We cannot offer a womb
to host your child,
but we can make our lives open
to receive your Spirit.

ALL: PLANT IN US WHAT YOU WILL,
CHANGE IN US WHAT YOU MUST,
UNTIL WE BEAR FRUIT TO YOUR GLORY,
THE KIND THAT LASTS FOR EVER.
AMEN.

Silence

Dismissal

Leader: Let us bless the Lord.
ALL: THANKS BE TO GOD.

Evening Liturgy D

The second prayer in this liturgy allows for worshippers to bring to mind the names of specific people. Let those who gather be aware of this before the liturgy begins and indicate whether the pauses will be silent or be times in which names (preferably first names) can be said aloud.

When this happens, the pause may extend for longer than 20 seconds, to let all who wish to contribute to be given time. The optional introductory chant is found on page 110.

Opening responses

Leader: Breath of God,
 breath of life,
 breath of deepest yearning.
ALL: COME, HOLY SPIRIT. *(Spoken or sung)*

Leader: Comforter,
 Disturber,
 Interpreter,
 Inspirer,
ALL: COME, HOLY SPIRIT. *(As above)*

Leader: Heavenly Friend,
 Lamplighter,
 Revealer of truth,
 Midwife of change,
ALL: COME, HOLY SPIRIT. *(As above)*

Leader: The Lord is here;
ALL: GOD'S SPIRIT IS WITH US.

Song *or* Hymn

Prayer

Leader A: Let us pray.

                Holy are you,
                God beyond all names,
                Life behind all being.

Leader B: Holy are you,
                greater than our best thought,
                deeper than our most profound experience,
                closer than our next breath.

ALL: HOLY ARE YOU,
                HIGH ABOVE THE UNIVERSE,
                ACCOMPANIED BY ANGEL SONG AND ETERNITY.

Leader A: We cannot tell you anything
                you do not already know;
                we cannot flatter you
                with what we do not understand;
                we cannot say
                what you have not given us the power to utter.

Leader B: But, in the mystery of your kindness,
                sometimes we feel summoned
                and sometimes we stumble
                into that holy ground
                where earth vibrates with heaven,
                and the hardest heart softens,
                and the most resistant will bends,
                and the soul long dumb or dormant cries glory.

ALL: LORD, MEET US HERE,
                FOR WE GATHER IN YOUR NAME
                AND CLAIM JESUS' PRESENCE
                AND WAIT FOR YOUR WORD.
                AMEN.

Psalm 90

Reader: Lord, you have been our refuge
 from one generation to another.
ALL: BEFORE THE MOUNTAINS EMERGED
 OR THE EARTH HAD BEEN BORN,
 YOU WERE AND ARE AND ALWAYS WILL BE
 GOD IN ETERNITY, HOLY AND ONE.

Reader: You turn back mortals to dust
 'Turn back, earth's children,' you say;
ALL: FOR IN YOUR SIGHT A THOUSAND YEARS
 ARE BUT A NIGHT WATCH OR A DAY.

Reader: So help us all to plan our years
 that wisdom may grow in our hearts.
ALL: SHOW US YOUR LOVE WHEN MORNING BREAKS,
 AND WE WILL BE JOYFUL ALL OF OUR DAYS.

A reading from Holy Scripture

Silence *and/ or* **Reflection** *(see page 12, section 5)*

Prayers for others

Leader: Let us hold before God in confidence ...

 ... the ones who laugh when we are funny,
 and the ones who make us smile at ourselves;

 (Pause)

 ... the ones for whom we weep,
 and the ones who, in joy or sorrow, weep for us;

 (Pause)

...the ones who worry that we may be lonely,
and the ones who ensure that does not happen;

(Pause)

...the ones who feed our minds and our bodies,
and the ones with whom we share faith
and break bread;

(Pause)

...the ones who reveal in themselves
what is hidden,
and the ones who treat as precious
all we confide in them.

(Pause)

...the ones who,
tonight,
we want to pray for,
and the ones who, unasked,
tonight will pray for us.

(Pause)

And let us thank God
for the one to whom we are summoned,
the one by whom we are sent,
whose image we are,
whose flesh we share,
whose love is all.

ALL: AMEN.

Song *or* **Hymn**

Closing responses

Leader: In life, in death, in life beyond death,
ALL: JESUS CHRIST IS LORD.

Leader: Over powers and authorities,
over all who govern the life of the world,
ALL: JESUS CHRIST IS LORD.

Leader: Of the poor, of the broken,
the sinned against and the sinner,
ALL:: JESUS CHRIST IS LORD.

Leader: Above the Church,
beyond our best thoughts of him,
and in the quietest corners of our hearts,
ALL: JESUS CHRIST IS LORD.

Leader: Thanks be to God.
ALL: AMEN.

Evening Liturgy E

The prayers for others in this liturgy arise from biblical quotations found in the psalms and the gospels. Open prayer may be offered after each section, or a silence for reflection may be observed. If a sung response is required, the refrain of the African American spiritual IT'S ME, O LORD may be appropriate.

Opening responses

Leader:	In light and in darkness,
	in peace and in confusion,
	Jesus Christ wants to make his home
	and meet his friends.
	He is the Light of Life:
ALL:	HE IS THE HOPE FOR THE WORLD.
Leader:	In him there is neither Jew nor Gentile,
	neither insider nor outsider;
ALL:	ALL ARE ONE IN JESUS CHRIST.
Leader:	He is the Light of Life:
ALL:	HE IS THE HOPE FOR THE WORLD.
Leader:	In him there is neither rich nor poor,
	neither black nor white;
ALL:	ALL ARE ONE IN JESUS CHRIST.
Leader:	He is the Light of Life:
ALL:	HE IS THE HOPE FOR THE WORLD.
Leader:	In him there is neither male nor female,
	neither master nor servant;
ALL:	ALL ARE ONE IN JESUS CHRIST.
Leader:	He is the Light of Life:
ALL:	HE IS THE HOPE FOR THE WORLD.

Song or **Hymn**

Prayer

Leader: Let us pray.

In the mystery of your presence,
no words are needed.
In the depth of your silence,
no sound is necessary.
In the face of your Word,
no voice need respond.

'Be still,' you say,
'and know that I am God.'

So, we will be still and listen …
    to the beating of our hearts,
    to the racing of our minds,
    to the pondering of our souls,
knowing that your Spirit, your Holy Spirit,
is beating, moving, provoking
within us and among us.

    (Pause)

And we will be still and listen …
    for the cry of the voiceless,
    for the groaning of the weary,
    for the pain of the wounded,
    for the sigh of the victim,
    for the laughter of children,
    for the song of gladness,
knowing that your Spirit, your Holy Spirit,
enables crying, groaning, sighing,
and also brings song and laughter.

    (Pause)

	We will be still,
	and if we do not take off our shoes,
	we will yet remember that this is Holy Ground
	because you have promised to be
	where your people meet in Jesus' name.
	So we will wait;
	patiently or impatiently
	we will wait
	for Jesus.
ALL:	AMEN.

Silence

Psalm 40

Leader:	I waited patiently for God
	and God bent down to hear me.
ALL:	GOD LIFTED ME FROM A MURKY PIT
	AND SET ME FIRMLY ON A ROCK
	WHERE I CAN STAND CONFIDENTLY.
Leader:	God put a new song on my lips,
	a song of praise to my Maker.
ALL:	MANY WILL LOOK ON IN WONDER
	AND PUT THEIR TRUST IN GOD.
Leader:	Countless are your wonders, O God;
	in goodness you have no equal.
ALL:	WE WOULD PROCLAIM ALL YOUR WORKS
	WERE THEY NOT TOO MANY TO NUMBER.

A reading from Holy Scripture

Silence *and/ or* **Reflection** *(see page 12, section 5)*

Prayers for others

Leader:　　Let us now, in prayer,
　　　　　　remember and call out to God
　　　　　　for those whom the following words of scripture
　　　　　　bring to mind.

　　　　　　Remember those
　　　　　　who tonight will cry,
　　　　　　'I wish to God it were morning,'
　　　　　　and come morning will cry,
　　　　　　'I wish to God it were night.'

　　　　　　　　(Silence and/ or sung response)

　　　　　　Remember those
　　　　　　whose pillows are soaked with tears
　　　　　　and whose eyes are tired and dim
　　　　　　with weeping.

　　　　　　　　(Silence and/ or sung response)

　　　　　　Remember those
　　　　　　who, for whatever reason,
　　　　　　may want to say,
　　　　　　'Jesus, remember me,
　　　　　　 when you come into your kingdom.'

　　　　　　　　(Silence and/ or sung response)

　　　　　　Remember those
　　　　　　for whom the light that was in them
　　　　　　has turned to darkness,
　　　　　　and that darkness is doubly dark.

　　　　　　　　(Silence and/ or sung response)

Remember those
who in looking to tomorrow,
deeply hope that
the sick will be healed,
the stranger welcomed,
the prisoner released,
the poor hear good news.

(Silence and/ or sung response)

And let us,
in confidence,
share with God our own hopes and longings.

(Silence and/ or sung response)

Glory to God our Maker,
to God's Son who is Christ our Lord,
to the Spirit who dwells in our hearts
both now and for ever.

ALL: AMEN.

Song *or* Hymn

Closing responses

Leader: God of Abraham and Sarah,
of Moses and Miriam,
of Mary and Joseph,
ALL: STAY WITH US NOW.

Leader: God of Joshua and Rahab,
of Rizpah and David,
of Dorcas and Paul,
ALL: STAY WITH US NOW.

Leader:	God of Simeon and Anna, of Martha and Thomas, God of the Eunuch at the Pool and the Woman at the Well,
ALL:	STAY WITH US NOW.
Leader:	Stay with us and go with us, for we leave as we gathered in Jesus' name.
ALL:	AMEN.

Evening Liturgy F

This liturgy draws on various texts from Carmina Gadelica. *See page 11, section 3.*

Opening responses

Leader: On the crest of the evening clouds,
behold the star-lighter at work.
ALL: OH, ALL YOU BRIGHT ANGELS IN HEAVEN,
SING PRAISES!

Leader: Great is God's love for the world,
proved in the gift of the Son.
ALL: OH, YOU WHO MAKE MUSIC ON EARTH,
SING PRAISES!

Leader: Christ of the loveliest Mary,
saviour and lover of all,
ALL: OUR HEARTS AND OUR VOICES CRY GLORY!
WE PRAISE YOU!

or

Opening meditation

Reader: I am the Gift, I am the Poor,
I am the Man of this night.

I am the Son seeking my siblings,
I have a cross on my shoulder.

I see angels heralding on high
and the dove coming with kindness towards me.

I am the host who stands at the lintel
of the door you alone can open.

Song *or* **Hymn**

Prayer

Leader: I will not lie down with evil;
ALL: NOR SHALL EVIL LIE DOWN WITH ME.

Leader: I will lie down with God;
ALL: AND GOD WILL LIE DOWN WITH ME.

Leader: Let us pray.

You are the Being of marvels,
the Keeper of our souls,
the Father of the naked,
the Ruler of the elements.

On land and sea,
in wild wind and warm welcome,
you embrace us,
ever present, watchful and kind.

Now as shadows lengthen and voices hush,
and the busyness of the day is set aside,
make this place a sheltering house
where we may rest in your presence
and remember the many blessings of this day:

(Pause, during which specific blessings may be mentioned aloud)

For your keeping of us,
your guidance to us,
your gospel for us,
receive our grateful prayer.

ALL:	THANKS BE TO YOU, O GOD, FOR EVERY GIFT YOU HAVE GIVEN: OUR THINKING, OUR SPEAKING, OUR DESIRE TO DO YOUR WILL, OUR HOPE TO ENTER YOUR KINGDOM. AND THANKS BE TO YOU FOR JESUS CHRIST OUR SAVIOUR, WHO HAS VISITED AND REDEEMED THE EARTH, AND FOR YOUR EVER-HOLY SPIRIT, WHO OPENS TO US THE DOORS TO TRUE FAITH, DEEP TRUTH AND HOLY WISDOM, AMEN.

Psalm 121

Reader:	If I lift up my eyes towards the hills, where will my help be found?
ALL:	YOUR HELP COMES FROM THE LORD, THE GOD WHO MADE HEAVEN AND EARTH.
Reader:	God will keep you from stumbling, your protector is always at hand.
ALL:	GOD KEEPS A WATCH ON ALL PEOPLE; GOD NEVER SLUMBERS OR SLEEPS.
Reader:	God is your keeper at all times; the Lord is at your right hand.
ALL:	IN SUNLIGHT NO HARM SHALL BEFALL YOU; IN MOONLIGHT YOUR LIFE IS SECURE.
Reader:	The Lord will guard you from evil; God will protect your soul.
ALL:	GOD WATCHES YOUR COMING AND GOING BOTH NOW AND FOR EVERMORE.

A reading from Holy Scripture

Silence *and/ or* **Reflection** *(see page 12, section 5)*

Night prayer

Leader: Let us pray.

                In your name, O Jesus, who was crucified
                we will lie down tonight,
                and give ourselves and all whom we love
                into your protection.

                (Pause)

ALL: LET NO THOUGHT COME TO OUR HEARTS,
                NO SOUND COME TO OUR EARS,
                NO TEMPTATION COME TO OUR EYES,
                NOR ANY TROUBLE
                COME TO OUR HOUSEHOLDS
                WHICH WOULD HURT OUR BODIES
                OR HARM OUR SOULS.

Leader: With your strong love surround us;
                and in our resting and our rising,
                nourish us and all whom we love
                with the health and happiness of heaven.

ALL: AMEN.

Song *or* Hymn

Closing responses

Leader: O Great Mystery of Mysteries,
star above stars,
word within the Word
who gave Jesus to sleep
even in danger,
command your kind angels
to encircle this night
our souls and our bodies.

And from the home of light
to the place where we rest
send your Spirit
to mend and tend
and write on our hearts
the promises of Jesus.

ALL: LET OURS BE THE PEACE OF OUR MAKER,
AND OURS BE THE PEACE OF THE SON,
AND OURS BE THE PEACE OF THE SPIRIT
THROUGHOUT THE DARKNESS,
UNTIL MORNING COMES.
AMEN.

A Liturgy for Holy Communion

This liturgy may be used on its own or following an act of worship such as a service of the Word. Local usage should apply for the means and words of distribution and whether the Celebrant partakes of communion before or after others.

Also optional, but suggested, is the passing of the peace after all have received communion. This is an ancient practice which celebrates that the peace is not chumminess among neighbours, but a gift from God mediated through Christ who is present in the sacrament.

Note that there are a number of options throughout this liturgy, some of which may be more appropriate than others.

Preface *(for alternative prefaces see page 93)*

Celebrant: Gathered round a table
is where Jesus so often met people …

… gathered round the table of Matthew,
   the table of Zacchaeus,
   the table of Simon,
   the table of Peter,
   the table of Lazarus
   and Martha and Mary,
   the tables of Joanna and Susannah …

… gathered round a table
where he could see people face to face,
listen to their stories, share their laughter.

And here,
we are gathered round a table
because this is where Jesus has promised to be
for those who want to meet him.

So accept his invitation
and feel welcome at this table.
Jesus Christ,
who here offers us a foretaste of eternal life,
invites you to be his guests.

Song *or* Hymn

The Story

Celebrant: What we do here, we do because it is Jesus' will.

For he it was who once, in an upstairs room,
sat at a meal with his disciples.

Reader: During the meal, he took bread.
And when he had blessed it,
he broke it,
and said to his disciples,
'This is my body. It is given for you.
Do this to remember me.'

Later in the meal, he took a cup of wine
and after he had given thanks he said,
'In this cup is the new relationship with God
made possible because of my death.
Drink it, all of you ... to remember me.'

Celebrant: So we will do as Jesus did.

We take this bread and this wine
the produce of the earth
and the work of human hands
through which Jesus has promised
to make himself known.

And as he said a prayer before sharing,
let us follow his example.

A Liturgy for Holy Communion

The Great Prayer

Celebrant: The Lord be with you.
ALL: AND ALSO WITH YOU.
Celebrant: Lift up your hearts.
ALL: WE LIFT THEM TO THE LORD.
Celebrant: Let us give thanks to the Lord our God.
ALL: IT IS RIGHT TO GIVE GOD THANKS AND PRAISE.

(for alternative prefaces, see page 93; and alternative communion prayers, see page 95)

Celebrant: It is right to praise you,
for you are the One from whom we came
and the One to whom we will return.

You conceived the universe,
wove the world together
and hold all life in your hand.

You watch us waking or sleeping,
you keep every tear that we shed,
you hear every prayer we make,
you know both our best and our worst
and you will not let us go.

So, with rain, wind and sunshine,
with all that moves in time with its Maker,
we praise you.

With angels and archangels,
with the saints from long ago,
with our loved ones
who are gathered round your heavenly table,
we praise you.

With the church throughout the world,
Orthodox and Lutheran, Catholic and Reformed,
with all who love Jesus and honour his name,
we praise you,
singing the hymn of your everlasting glory:

Sanctus *(Spoken or sung)*

ALL: HOLY, HOLY, HOLY LORD
GOD OF POWER AND MIGHT;
HEAVEN AND EARTH
ARE FULL OF YOUR GLORY.
HOSANNA IN THE HIGHEST.

BLESSED IS HE   *(or THE ONE)*
WHO COMES IN THE NAME OF THE LORD.
HOSANNA IN THE HIGHEST.

Celebrant: Yes, blessed is he ...

who was born among us incognito,
who grew up without privilege or status,
who walked the way to heaven
    through the back streets of this world,
who told the deepest truths
    in ordinary language,
who touched and healed, blessed and disturbed
    without fear or favour,
who showed inclusive love
    in all its unconditional glory;
who, for all this, was crucified, died and was buried,
who, for all this and for all of us, rose again;
who, though high in heaven,
is present with us
here and now.

Blessed is he in all his love and beauty.

God beyond holiness,
as we do what Jesus once did,
let your Spirit move among us
to settle on this bread and this wine
that they may become for us
the body and blood of Christ.

And let that same Spirit stir our souls
so that as we share this sacrament,
we may recognise our Lord and receive him
that he may be in us and we in him for ever.
Amen.

The Fraction

Celebrant: Among friends,
gathered round a table,
Jesus took bread;
and when he had blessed it,
he broke it and said,

'Take this and eat it.

It is my body.
It is given for you.

Do this to remember me.'

Then later, during the meal,
he took a cup of wine,
and when he had given thanks, he said,

'In this cup is the new relationship with God
made possible because of my death.

Take this, all of you,
to remember me.'

(The Celebrant may partake here or later)

Invitation

All you who hunger and thirst
    for a better life,
    for a deeper faith,
    for a better world,
here is the bread of life:
    feed on it with gratitude;
here is the cup of salvation
    drink from it and believe.

The gifts of God for the people of God.

(For alternative, seasonal invitational sentences, see page 100)

Communion

The Peace

Celebrant: The angels said it to startled shepherds
and Jesus said it to frightened followers.
And now these words which come from heaven
are shared to make us whole and make us one:

Peace be with you
ALL: AND ALSO WITH YOU.

(The peace is shared according to local practice)

Dismissal

Celebrant: Go now, you have been fed,
you have shared the living bread;
you have been grafted to the vine,
you have tasted heaven's new wine.

Go now, you have been blessed.
Jesus called you each his guest.
God knows your name and says you're wanted
and in your lives God's seed is planted.

Go now, and go in Christ's own peace
and in your going do not cease
to love yourself – you are God's treasure,
and love the world – it is God's pleasure,
and love the Lord in greatest measure.
Amen.

Song *or* **Hymn**

Blessing *or* **Benediction** *(According to local practice)*

....

Alternative Prefaces

1.

A follower of Jesus once wrote:
'Think what kind of people you are
whom God has called:
not many wise by human standards,
not many powerful or of noble birth.
Yet to shame the wise,
God has chosen what the world counts foolish;
and to shame the strong,
God has chosen what the world counts weak.'

It is not for our virtue
that we are here.
It is not for who we are
that we are called to this table.

It is only for one reason –
that God wants us.

So come,
leaving behind the baggage of your self-importance
or the burden of your self-loathing.
How you feel,
who you are,
what you have done,
at this moment does not matter.

There is a greater cause,
there is a stronger voice.
It belongs to Jesus who, in bread and wine, says,
'I am here ... for you.'

2.

This is the second-last table Jesus prepared.

For, at the Last Supper, he spoke of a time
when he would again meet around a table
with his disciples.
This sacrament, therefore, is a foretaste
of what is to come.

In heaven, where all the ambiguities of life
are no longer puzzling,
in heaven, when all the regrets of life
no longer hurt,
in heaven, where all the deep joys of life
find their fulfilment,
in heaven, where all that has been repented
is known to be forgiven,
in heaven ...
we will sit and sing, eat and drink
in the glorious company of Jesus
who has gone to prepare that final table.

But on earth, we are given this table
which he has also prepared
so that we might meet him and he meet us
in this world and in this time,
in the mystery of bread and wine
which will keep us bound to him
in eternal life.

....

Alternative communion prayers

1. (Reflecting the ministry of Jesus)

Yes, it is right to give you thanks and praise
for the life you lived among us,
speaking our language,
learning our ways,
sitting at our tables,
listening to our complaints
and never giving up on us,
never giving up on us.

Yes, it is right to give you thanks and praise
for never compromising the truth by which you lived,
for refusing to be swayed by popular opinion,
for identifying the seductions of power,
for confronting institutionalised prejudice
and never selling your soul,
never selling your soul.

Yes, it is right to give you thanks and praise
for loving the unlovable,
touching the untouchable,
forgiving the unforgivable,
recognising the gold beneath the dross,
the potential beneath the pain,
and never taking an easier path,
never taking an easier path.

Yes it is right to give you thanks and praise
for in the face of our small-mindedness
you, Jesus, have shown us God and God's kingdom
in fascinating beauty and converting power.

So we gladly celebrate your life,
as in concert with the church in heaven and earth
we join the song of your unending praise.

> HOLY, HOLY, HOLY LORD
> GOD OF POWER AND MIGHT;
> HEAVEN AND EARTH
> ARE FULL OF YOUR GLORY.
> HOSANNA IN THE HIGHEST.
>
> BLESSED IS HE   (or THE ONE)
> WHO COMES IN THE NAME OF THE LORD.
> HOSANNA IN THE HIGHEST.

Oh, Holy Jesus,
it is not by virtue that we are here,
but by your gracious invitation.

It is not to continue an ancient tradition
but to be nourished by our living Lord.

It is not only to celebrate your presence among us
but to catch a glimpse of heaven,
because, in this sacrament,
you give us a foretaste of that heavenly banquet
where we shall see you face to face
and enjoy the freedom of eternity
when the limitations of earth are no more.

God our Maker,
as you gave your people water
from a rock in the desert
and fed them with bread in the wilderness,
let your Holy Spirit
fill this bread and this wine

with the fullness of Jesus
so that we, in stretching out our hands,
receive, through faith, food for our souls.

In the intimacy of this sacrament,
as heaven and earth become one,
enable us to know you more deeply
and resolve to love, honour and serve you
more faithfully in this world,
until your kingdom comes.
Amen.

(Return to Fraction on page 91)

2. *(Reflecting the song of the earth)*

We do well to praise you,
and in this we are not alone.

Every atom proclaims your glory;
the smallest creature and highest mountain
both attest to your creative genius;
the stunning climax of great music
and the trusting grasp of a child's hand
bear witness to your love.

Though we cannot hear them,
the valleys sing for joy.

Though we do not see them,
the hills skip like lambs.

Though we seldom notice it,
all of creation daily performs a symphony
for your delight.

And we, also the work of your hand,
are helplessly caught up in this universal anthem.

So, with the valleys and the hills,
with nature in all its harmony and discord,
we sing.

With people in every land
and languages of every nation,
we sing.

With those who once sat beside us
and now are guests at your banquet in heaven,
we sing.

With the angels and the saints
who cannot keep silent,
for you are always present,
we sing.

With them we sing the song of your everlasting glory.

> HOLY, HOLY, HOLY LORD
> GOD OF POWER AND MIGHT;
> HEAVEN AND EARTH
> ARE FULL OF YOUR GLORY.
> HOSANNA IN THE HIGHEST.
>
> BLESSED IS HE   (or THE ONE)
> WHO COMES IN THE NAME OF THE LORD.
> HOSANNA IN THE HIGHEST.

Now, Holy God,
lest we believe that what we have to offer
is more than you have to give,
we remember with reverence
the one who is both our host and our saviour.

Born into obscurity,
flesh of our flesh,
bone of our bone he came.

Baptised into solidarity with all
who yearn for a better world,
touching those whose disease might contaminate him,
dining with those whose company might discredit him;
flesh of our flesh,
bone of our bone he came.

Identifying the uniqueness in all who were ordinary,
transforming dead tradition into living faith,
comforting and confronting,
healing and disturbing,
flesh of our flesh,
bone of our bone he came.

And then denied by those who followed him,
crucified by those who feared him,
dead, buried, consigned to hell
until heaven required his resurrection
and he arose to redeem all that we had ruined;
flesh of our flesh,
bone of our bone,
him we hallow,
whose name is Jesus.

Holy and gracious God,
present with us now,
send in kindness your Holy Spirit
to settle on this bread and wine
and fill them with the fullness of Jesus.

And as we share this holy food,
may that same Spirit nourish, cherish and change us
until through the mystery of your grace,
we know ourselves to be
flesh of his flesh, bone of his bone,
and resolve to love and follow Christ for ever.
Amen.

(return to Fraction on page 91)

Alternative invitational sentences

Advent

He who was with God in the beginning,
comes to us in this bread.
He of whom the prophets spoke
is present to us in this cup.

Christmas

As Mary's body was given for Jesus,
so Jesus' body is given for us.
Here the Word made flesh
comes to us,
cradled in bread and in wine.

Epiphany

As Jesus revealed his glory
to people from near and far
at his birth and his baptism,
so, to those who seek him,
he offers himself here and now
in bread and wine.

Lent

Behold the Lamb of God.
He who takes away the sin of the world
forgives, restores and embraces us
in this bread and this cup.

Easter

He who was buried but rose from the dead
is present to us in this bread.
He, whose wounded hands
were offered to the unbelieving,
reaches out to us in this cup.

Ascension & Pentecost

The One who promised to be with us
to the end of the world,
keeps his promise in this bread.
The One whose Spirit descended on his disciples
with startling power,
embraces us in this cup.

Marriage

The One who was pleased to be present
at the wedding of friends,
is present to us in this bread.
The One whose word turned water into wine
comes lovingly to us in this cup.

Funeral

The One who grieved deeply
for the death of his friend
shares his solidarity with us in this bread.
The One who has prepared a place for us in heaven
offers his consolation in this cup.

Appendix

A: Affirmations of Belief

These affirmations may be used as and where appropriate. See note on page 12.

      1. Affirming the Trinitarian

Leader: We believe in God;
ALL: WHO IS OLDER THAN ETERNITY
AND YOUNGER THAN OUR NEXT BREATH;
WHO IS BEYOND DESCRIBING
YET KNOWS US ALL BY NAME;
WHO INSPIRES FAITH
YET CANNOT BE CONTAINED BY RELIGION.

Leader: We believe in Jesus Christ,
flesh of our flesh, bone of our bone;
ALL: HE CAME IN THE BODY
TO GIVE WORTH TO EVERY HUMAN LIFE.
HE TOUCHED THE UNTOUCHABLE,
LOVED THE UNLOVABLE,
FORGAVE THE UNFORGIVABLE
AND ENDURED SLANDER,
PERSECUTION AND DEATH
IN ORDER THAT THROUGH SUFFERING LOVE
GOD'S KINGDOM MIGHT COME ON EARTH.

HE ROSE FROM THE GRAVE AS LIVING PROOF
THAT WHAT IS LAID DOWN IN FAITH
WILL BE RAISED IN GLORY.
HE ASCENDED TO HEAVEN
THAT HE MIGHT BE PRESENT
AT ALL TIMES
TO ALL PEOPLE.

Appendix A: Affirmations of Belief

Leader: We believe in the Holy Spirit,
ALL: WHO LEADS US INTO TRUTH AND FREEDOM,
WHO GIVES GOOD GIFTS
TO ALL GOD'S CHILDREN,
WHO INSPIRES RESEARCH, ENABLES PRAYER,
AND WILLS
THAT HUMAN ECONOMICS AND POLITICS
SHOULD PRIORITISE JUSTICE,
CARE OF THE EARTH
AND THE HEALING OF THE NATIONS.

Leader: We celebrate the potential of the Church,
ALL: THE LIFE IN OUR BODIES,
THE YEARNING IN OUR SOULS,
THE PROMISE OF GOOD THINGS IN STORE
FOR THOSE WHO LOVE THE LORD.

2. Affirming the Global Church

Leader: We believe in God,
ALL: WHO BEFRIENDED A WANDERING PEOPLE,
CALLING THEM FROM SLAVERY INTO FREEDOM;
YET WHO IN RAHAB, TAMAR,
RUTH, BATHSHEBA,
CYRUS, DARIUS AND MANY OTHERS
CALLED OUTSIDERS
TO BE AGENTS OF GOD'S PURPOSE.

Leader: We believe in Jesus,
ALL: WHO WAS REVERED BY PERSIAN SAGES,
SOUGHT AND FOUND ASYLUM IN EGYPT,
PREACHED THE LOVE OF GOD TO SYRIANS,
ATTRACTED GREEKS TO HIS CAUSE,
FOUND HIS FIRST EVANGELIST IN A SAMARITAN,
SAW INCOMPARABLE FAITH IN A ROMAN,
HAD HIS CROSS SHOULDERED BY A LIBYAN,
AND ASCENDED ABOVE HIS NATIVE LAND
THAT HE MIGHT BE PRESENT IN ALL PLACES.

Leader: We believe in the Holy Spirit,
ALL: WHO AT PENTECOST PROVED THAT HEAVEN
HAS NO FAVOURED MOTHER-TONGUE;
WHO, IN THE BAPTISM OF AN ETHIOPIAN,
DENIED RACISM A FOOTHOLD IN FAITH;
AND WHO,
IN THE ANCIENT AND MODERN WORLDS,
FOUNDED CHURCHES IN DIFFERENT CULTURES.

Leader: We believe that God is supremely known in Jesus.
ALL: YET WE AFFIRM
THAT GOD IS PRESENT AMONG PEOPLE
WHO DO NOT OWN CHRIST AS THEIR LORD.

Leader: We believe that the kingdom of God
is bigger than the Church,
and that the love of God
is beyond our understanding.
ALL: THEREFORE WE CELEBRATE
THAT GOD'S WAYS ARE NOT OUR WAYS,
THAT GOD KNOWS WHOM GOD CHOOSES,
AND RESERVES THE RIGHT
TO SURPASS ALL HUMAN EXPECTATION.

BLESSED BE GOD FOR EVER.

3. Affirming the Church's Mission

Leader: That we worship one God,
Father, Son and Holy Spirit,
in whose image we are made,
to whose service we are summoned,
by whose presence we are renewed:
ALL: THIS WE BELIEVE.

Appendix A: Affirmations of Belief

Leader: That it is central to the mission of Christ
that we participate through word and action
to rejoice in the diversity of human culture,
to preserve the earth
in all its beauty and frailty,
to witness to the love of God
for every person,
and to invite all to share
in that converting experience:
ALL: THIS WE BELIEVE.

Leader: That through the power of the Holy Spirit,
the persecuted shall be lifted up
and the wicked will fall,
the heartfelt prayers
and hidden actions of God's people
shall change for good the course of human history,
the ancient words of scripture
shall continue to startle us
with fresh insight:
ALL: THIS WE BELIEVE.

Leader: That God has called the Church into being
to be the servant of the kingdom,
to be a sign of God's new order,
to celebrate in every land
worship which raises our hearts to heaven:
ALL: THIS WE BELIEVE.

Leader: That Christ, fully aware of our differences,
prays that we may be one
so that the world may believe:
ALL: THIS WE BELIEVE
AND TO THIS WE ARE COMMITTED
FOR THE LOVE OF GOD,
IN THE WAY OF CHRIST,
BY THE POWER OF THE HOLY SPIRIT.

4. Celebrating the Ministry of Jesus

Group A:	He is among us:
	the one who gave sight to the blind
	and insight to the closed-minded;
Group B:	the one who gave hearing to the deaf
	and listening ears to those
	who heard only their own voices.
ALL:	THE ONE WHO MADE THE LAME WALK
	AND IS THE WAY, THE TRUTH AND THE LIFE.
Group A:	He is among us:
	the one who healed the sick
	and helped the hopeless;
Group B:	the one who exorcised demons
	and gave new names to those
	who were known only for their problems,
ALL:	THE ONE WHO WAS CRITICISED
	FOR COMING TOO CLOSE
	TO THE CONTAMINATED.
Group A:	He is among us:
	the one who agreed with fair taxation
	and handled money;
Group B:	the one who spoke for the poor
	and who spoke to the privileged
	of the good things their wealth could do,
ALL:	THE ONE
	WHO ENTRUSTED HIMSELF TO WOMEN
	AS MUCH AS MEN,
	WITHOUT PREJUDICE OR FAVOUR.
Group A:	He is among us
	to touch, to heal,
Group B:	to bless, to inspire,
Group A:	to confront, to convert,
Group B:	to show at all times
	the human face of God.
ALL:	HE IS AMONG US.

B: Songs

Come, bring your burdens to God

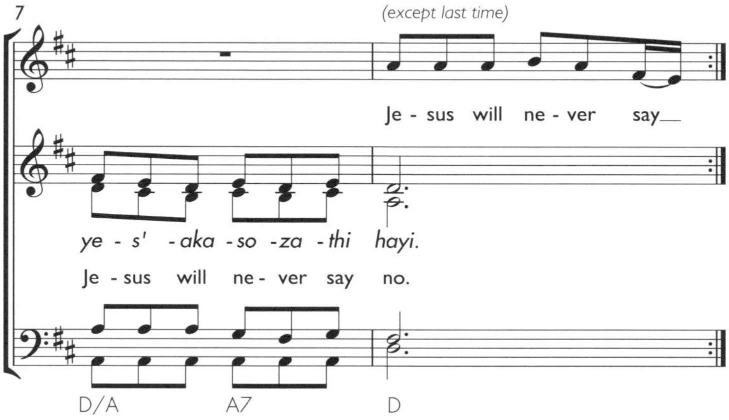
7
(except last time)
Je - sus will ne - ver say
ye - s' - aka - so - za - thi hayi.
Je - sus will ne - ver say no.
D/A A7 D

Words & melody South African traditional; arrangement copyright © Welile Sigabi, South Africa (transcribed by Barbara Clark, Mairi Munro & Martine Stemerick, from the singing of the Mooiplas congregation).

Gloria (Iona)

solemnly
Glo - ri - a, Glo - ri - a, Glo - ri - a,
4
in ex - cel - sis De - o.

Words & music Scottish traditional liturgical.

Appendix B: Songs

Come, Holy Spirit

Appendix B: Songs

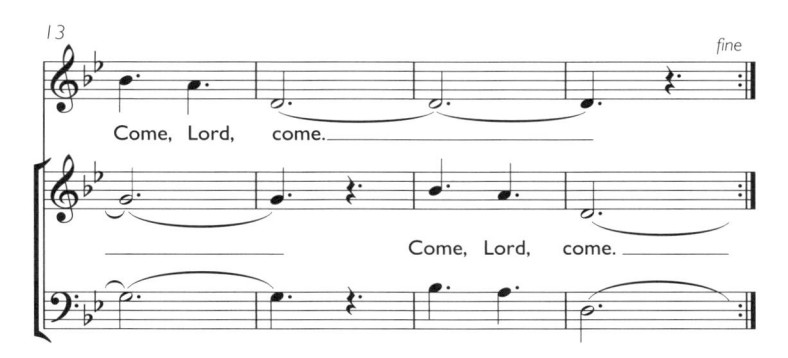

Come, Lord, come.
Come, Lord, come.

Words & music John L. Bell, copyright © 1995 WGRG, Iona Community, Glasgow G2 3DH, Scotland. www.wgrg.co.uk

Through our lives and by our prayers

gently

Through our lives and by our prayers, your Kingdom come.

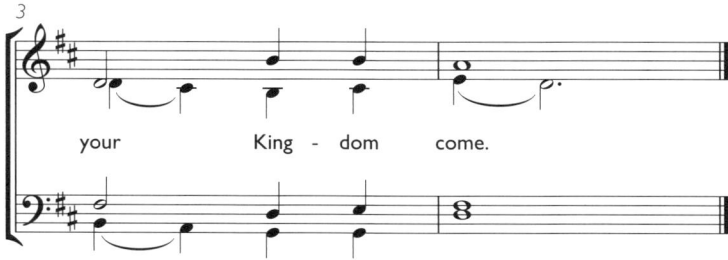

Words & music John L. Bell, copyright © 2012 WGRG, Iona Community, Glasgow G2 3DH, Scotland. www.wgrg.co.uk

Appendix B: Songs

Alleluia (Greenbelt 10)

tenderly ♩ = 60

(AL-LE-LU-IA, AL-LE-LU-IA, AL-LE-LU-IA, AL-LE-LU-IA. AL-LE-LU-IA, AL-LE-LU-IA, AL-LE-LU-IA, AL-LE-LU-IA.)

Words & music John L. Bell, copyright © 2012 WGRG, Iona Community, Glasgow G2 3DH, Scotland. www.wgrg.co.uk

Kyrie (Maurs)

Words & music John L. Bell, copyright © 2008 WGRG, Iona Community, Glasgow G2 3DH, Scotland. www.wgrg.co.uk

Glory and gratitude and praise

firmly

Glo - ry and gra - ti - tude and praise
now let earth to hea - ven raise.
Glo - ry and gra - ti - tude and praise:

Appendix B: Songs

these we offer to God.

Words & music John L. Bell, copyright © 1998 WGRG, Iona Community, Glasgow G2 3DH, Scotland. www.wgrg.co.uk

On God alone I wait silently

quietly

On God alone I wait silently; God my deliverer, God my strong tower.

Paraphrase (Ps.62) & music John L. Bell, copyright © 1993 WGRG, Iona Community, Glasgow G2 3DH, Scotland. www.wgrg.co.uk

Peace I leave

as the mood requires ♩ = 56

Peace I leave, my peace I give you, not the peace the world can of-fer. In each storm, in each con-fu-sion I'll be with you.

Words & music John L. Bell, copyright © 2012 WGRG, Iona Community, Glasgow G2 3DH, Scotland. www.wgrg.co.uk

Appendix B: Songs

Take, O take me as I am

gently

Take, O take me as I am;
sum-mon out what I shall be;
set your seal up-on my heart and live in me.

Words & music John L. Bell, copyright © 1995 WGRG, Iona Community, Glasgow G2 3DH, Scotland. www.wgrg.co.uk

Listen, Lord

gently

Lis-ten, Lord, lis-ten, Lord, not to our words but to our prayer. You a-lone, you a-lone un-der-stand and care.

Words & music John L. Bell, & Graham Maule, copyright © 1989 WGRG, Iona Community, Glasgow G2 3DH, Scotland. www.wgrg.co.uk

This is the Body of Christ

gently

This is the body of Christ, broken that we may be whole; this cup, as promised by God, true to his word, cradles our Lord: food for the good of the soul.

Words & music John L. Bell, copyright © 1998 WGRG, Iona Community, Glasgow G2 3DH, Scotland. www.wgrg.co.uk

Appendix B: Songs

Come to me

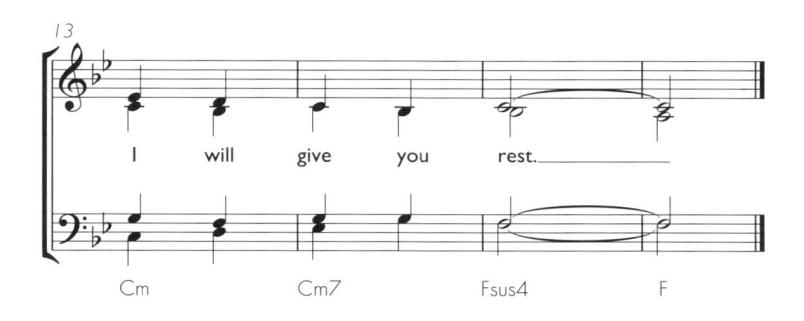

Words & music John L. Bell, copyright © 2008 WGRG, Iona Community, Glasgow G2 3DH, Scotland. www.wgrg.co.uk

Listen to the Word

Words & music Canadian source unknown © copyright control.

The Wild Goose Resource Group

The Wild Goose Resource Group is a semi-autonomous project of the Iona Community, committed to the renewal of public worship. Based in Glasgow, the WGRG has three resource workers, John Bell, Jo Love and Graham Maule, who lead workshops, seminars and events throughout Britain and abroad. They are supported by Gail Ullrich, who fulfils the role of the Group's administrator.

The task of the WGRG has been to develop and identify new methods and materials to enable the revitalisation of congregational song, prayer and liturgy. Songs and liturgical material have been translated and used in many countries across the world as well as being frequently broadcast on radio and television. From time to time, the Wild Goose Collective – an ad hoc assortment of singers associated with the Group – record new songs by WGRG.

The WGRG, along with a committed group of fellow-Glaswegians, run *Holy City*, a monthly ecumenical workshop and worship event for adults in the centre of Glasgow.

The WGRG also publish a mail-order catalogue, an annual Liturgy Booklet series as well as a twice-yearly newsletter, *GOOSEgander*, to enable friends and supporters to keep up to date with WGRG developments.

If you would like to find out more about subscribing to these, or about ways to support the WGRG financially, please contact:

Wild Goose Resource Group,
Iona Community, 21 Carlton Court,
Glasgow G5 9JP, Scotland.

Tel: 0141 429 7281
E-mail: wildgoose@wildgoose.scot
Web: www.wildgoose.scot (for information and online sales)
www.holycity-glasgow.co.uk
Twitter: 'WildGooseRG' / 'HolyCityGlasgow'
Facebook: 'Wild Goose Resource Group' / 'Holy City Glasgow'

Wild Goose Resource Group Titles

SONGBOOKS, ANTHEM PACKS & CDs

Come All You People – Short songs for worship, Vol.1, John L. Bell & Wild Goose Worship Group. Book: ISBN 9780947988685 / CD: 9781901557404.
Courage To Say No, The – Twenty three songs for Lent & Easter, John L. Bell & Graham Maule & Wild Goose Worship Group. Book: ISBN 9780947988784; CD: ISBN 9781901557442.
Enemy Of Apathy – Wild Goose Songs, Vol.2, John L. Bell & Graham Maule & Wild Goose Worship Group. Book: ISBN 9780947988272.
God Comes Tomorrow, John L. Bell & The Cathedral Singers. Anthem Pack: GIA G-4376; CD: GIA CD-494.
God Never Sleeps, John L. Bell & The Cathedral Singers. Anthem Pack: GIA G-4376; CD: GIA CD-348.
Heaven Shall Not Wait – Wild Goose Songs, Vol.1, John L. Bell & Graham Maule & Wild Goose Worship Group. Book: ISBN 9781901557800; CD ISBN 9781901557459.
I Will Not Sing Alone – Songs for the seasons of love, John L. Bell & Wild Goose Collective. Book: 9781901557916; CD: ISBN 9781901557893.
Innkeepers & Light Sleepers – 17 songs for Christmas, John L. Bell & Wild Goose Worship Group. Book: ISBN 9780947988470; CD: ISBN 9781901557398.
Last Journey, The, John L. Bell & The Cathedral Singers. Book: GIA G-4527P; Anthem Pack: GIA G-4527; CD: GIA CD-381.
Love & Anger – Songs of lively faith and social justice, John L. Bell & Graham Maule & Wild Goose Worship Group. Book: ISBN 9780947988982; CD: ISBN 9781901557411.
Love From Below – Wild Goose Songs, Vol.3, John L. Bell & Graham Maule & Wild Goose Worship Group. Book: ISBN 0 947988 34 3; CD: ISBN 9781901557466.
One Is The Body – Songs of unity and diversity, John L. Bell & Wild Goose Worship Group. Book: ISBN 9781901557350; CD: ISBN 9781901557374.

Psalms Of Patience, Protest & Praise – 23 Psalm settings, John L. Bell & Wild Goose Worship Group. Book: ISBN 9780947988562; CD: ISBN 9780947988579.
Seven Psalms Of David, John L. Bell. Anthem Pack: GIA G-4830.
Seven Songs Of Mary, John L. Bell. Book: GIA G-4652.
Seven Songs Of Mary & Seven Psalms of David, John L. Bell & The Cathedral Singers. CD: GIA CD-403
Splendour Of The House Of God, The, John L. Bell. & The Cathedral Singers. Anthem Pack: GIA G-8099; CD: GIA CD-874.
There Is One Among Us – Short songs for worship, Vol.2, John L. Bell & Wild Goose Worship Group. Book: ISBN 9781901557107; CD: 9781901557213.
Take This Moment, John L. Bell & The Cathedral Singers. Anthem Pack: GIA G-5155; CD: GIA CD-464.
Truth That Sets Us Free, The – Biblical songs for worship, John L. Bell & Wild Goose Collective. Book: ISBN 9781849522304; CD: ISBN 9781849522403.
We Walk His Way – Short songs for worship, Vol.3, John L. Bell & Wild Goose Collective. Book: ISBN 9781905010554; CD: ISBN 9781905010424.
When Grief is Raw – Songs for times of sorrow & bereavement, John L. Bell & Graham Maule. Book: ISBN 9780947988913.

SONG METHODOLOGY

Singing Thing, The – A case for congregational song, John L. Bell. Book: ISBN 9781901557282.
Singing Thing Too, The – Enabling congregations to sing, John L. Bell. Book: ISBN 9781905010325.

RESOURCE BOOKS

Cloth For The Cradle – Worship resources and readings for Advent, Christmas & Epiphany, Wild Goose Worship Group. Book: ISBN 9781901557015.
He Was In The World – Meditations for public worship, John L Bell. Book: ISBN 9780947988708.

Jesus & Peter – Off-the-record conversations, John L. Bell & Graham Maule. Book: ISBN 9781901557176.
Present On Earth – Worship resources on the life of Jesus, Wild Goose Worship Group. Book: ISBN 9781901557640.
Stages On The Way – Worship resources for Lent, Holy Week & Easter, Wild Goose Worship Group. Book: ISBN 9781901557114 **Wee Worship Book, A** – 4th Incarnation, John L. Bell, Mairi Munro & Wild Goose Resource Group. Book: ISBN 9781901557190.

THEOLOGICAL REFLECTIONS

10 Things They Never Told Me About Jesus – A beginner's guide to a larger Christ, John L. Bell. Book: ISBN 9781905010608.
All That Matters – Collected scripts from Radio 4's Thought for The Day, Vol.2, John L. Bell. Book: ISBN 9781849520706.
Hard Words For Interesting Times – Biblical texts in contemporary contexts, John L. Bell. Book: ISBN 9781901557756.
States Of Bliss & Yearning – The marks and means of authentic Christian spirituality, John L. Bell. Book: ISBN 9781901557077.
Thinking Out Loud – Collected scripts from Radio 4's Thought for The Day, Vol.1, John L. Bell. Book: ISBN 9781905010417.

WGRG LITURGY BOOKLETS

Spare Change & Gilt-Edged Grace – A liturgy exploring the relationship between faith and wealth, Wild Goose Resource Group. Liturgy Booklet no.12; ISBN 9781909469112.
God & Her Girls – A celebration of the giftedness of forgotten women, Wild Goose Resource Group. Liturgy Booklet no.11; ISBN 9781909469105.
Harvesting The World – A liturgy for harvest festivals, Wild Goose Resource Group. Liturgy Booklet no.10; ISBN 9781909469099.
Family Affair, A – A liturgy based on Jesus' most famous parable (the Prodigal Son), Wild Goose Resource Group. Liturgy

Booklet no.9; ISBN 9781909469082.
Fencing In God's People – A liturgy on 3000 years of wall building in Israel & Palestine, Wild Goose Resource Group. Liturgy Booklet no.8; ISBN 9781909469075.
Road To Roam, A – A way of celebrating sacred space, Wild Goose Resource Group. Liturgy Booklet no.7; ISBN 9781909469068.
Sweet Honey & Hard Places – Prayer services based on the Psalms, Wild Goose Resource Group; Liturgy Booklet no.6; ISBN 9781909469051.
Pictures Of God – An act of worship about images, Wild Goose Resource Group. Liturgy Booklet no.5; ISBN 9781909469044.
Remember Me Today – A Holy Week reflection, Wild Goose Resource Group. Liturgy Booklet no.4; ISBN 9781909469037.
Love Which Heals, The – A service of grieving & gratitude for those recently bereft, Wild Goose Resource Group. Liturgy Booklet no.3; ISBN 9781909469020.
Jubilee Liturgy, A – A liturgy for justice at the Millennium, Wild Goose Resource Group. Liturgy Booklet no.2; ISBN 9781909469013.
St Columba Of Iona – An order for the commemoration of the saint's life, Wild Goose Resource Group. Liturgy Booklet no.1; ISBN 9781909469006.

Order online at www.wgrg.co.uk or www.ionabooks.com